RARE LIFETIME COLLECTIONS PRESENTS...

The Beatles and Their Solo Years

A Trip Down Memory Lane

BY Tom Fontaine

© Copyright 2018, Tom Fontaine

All Rights Reserved.

In accordance with the U.S. Copyright Act of 1976, the scanning, uploading, and electronic sharing of any part of this book without the permission of the publisher constitute unlawful privacy and theft of the author's intellectual property. If you would like to use material from the book (other than for preview purposes), prior written permission must be obtained by contacting the publisher at the address below. Thank you for your support of the author's rights.

ISBN: 978-1-948638-88-3

ALL THE ITEMS PICTURED IN THIS BOOK WERE OWNED BY COLLECTOR TOM FONTAINE.

Table of Contents

THE BEATLES 1

JOHN LENNON 47

PAUL McCARTNEY 79

MY MEMORIES OF BEATLEFEST 119

GEORGE HARRISON................... 131

RINGO STARR 149

STUART SUTCLIFFE 163

EPILOGUE 169

Introduction

Hi, and welcome to Rare Lifetime Collections. When I wrote my first book titled *Rare, The Memorabilia Collection of a Lifetime* released in 2016, I was only able to share a glimpse into the Archive Section of the items I once owned in my over 50 years of collecting, which I am most proud of accomplishing. I received positive feedback and enquiries to see more after the first book.

This inspired me to create *The Beatles and Their Solo Years — A Trip Down Memory Lane*. The Four Lads from Liverpool were the obvious choice for me to share with you, the reader, as they were the music group that started it all for me as a collector way back in 1964.

Some of the pictures herein are high quality, while others were taken with older cameras, scanned with less than high quality scanners, etc. because that was what was available at the time. I guess you would say this is an illustrated history of my memories of collecting The Beatles memorabilia, and it is a great reference and study of their signatures over the years.

As you peruse these pages, you will encounter items seen in print, in other collections, in previous auctions and in museums. This book was created to continue the story of my experiences as a collector in words and images, highlighted with special features and personal memories. Looking back now, I am amazed how intensely I pursued collecting these incredible items, but it was all worth it. I'm excited to have the chance to share it with readers and fans, both old and new, of The Beatles.

Thanks to my family and friends who have supported me and my collecting through the years.

I hope readers will enjoy this book for many years to come.

Cheers!
Tom Fontaine, June 2018

THE BEATLES SHOW

presented by
JOHN SMITH

THE BEATLES

6.5 x 4.75 Photo of John Lennon with his first band The Quarrymen with a rare set of signatures by the original members (minus John) featuring (from left to right from the picture above) Eric Griffiths, Colin Hanton, Rod Davis, Pete Shotton, and Len Garry.

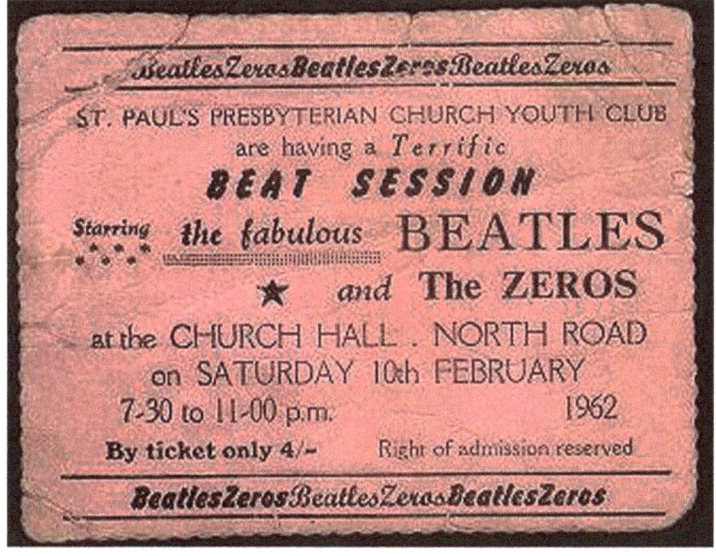

The Beatles signed ticket at St Paul's Presbyterian Church Hall Saturday February 10th, 1962

THE BEATLES

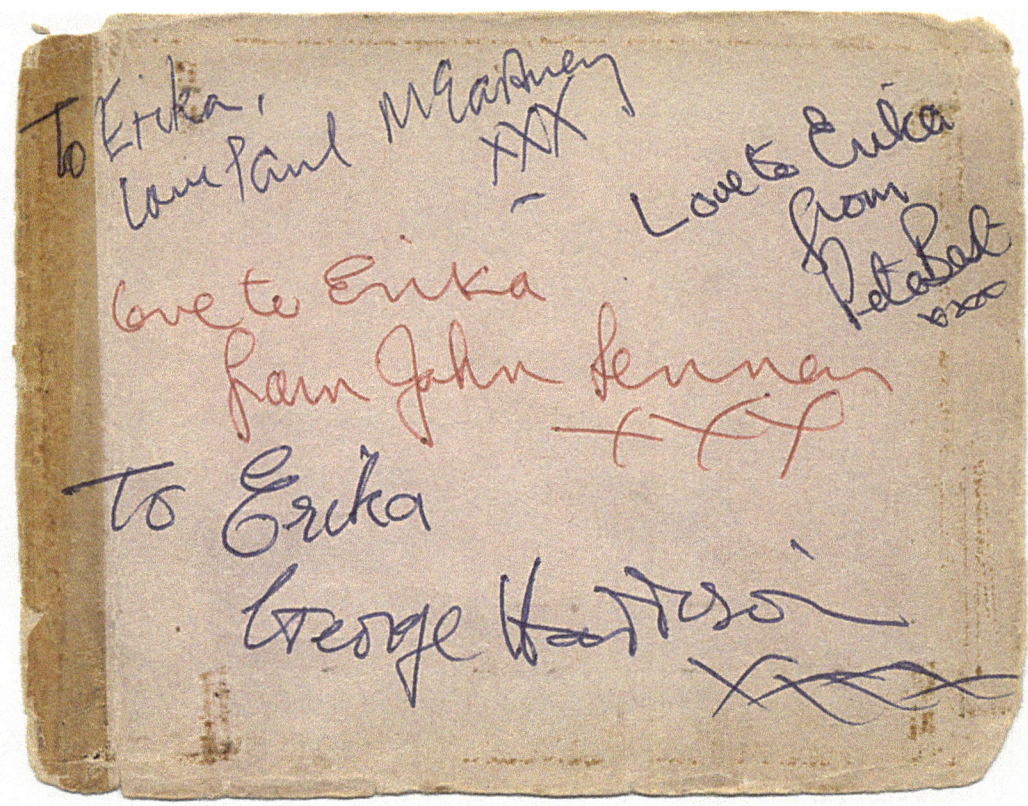

A very rare signature ensemble featuring The Beatles with Pate Best signed at the Cavern Club in early 1962 and on the reverse by Rory Storm's drummer Ringo Starr(before joining The Beatles) and later John Lennon's sons, Julian and Sean in 1998.

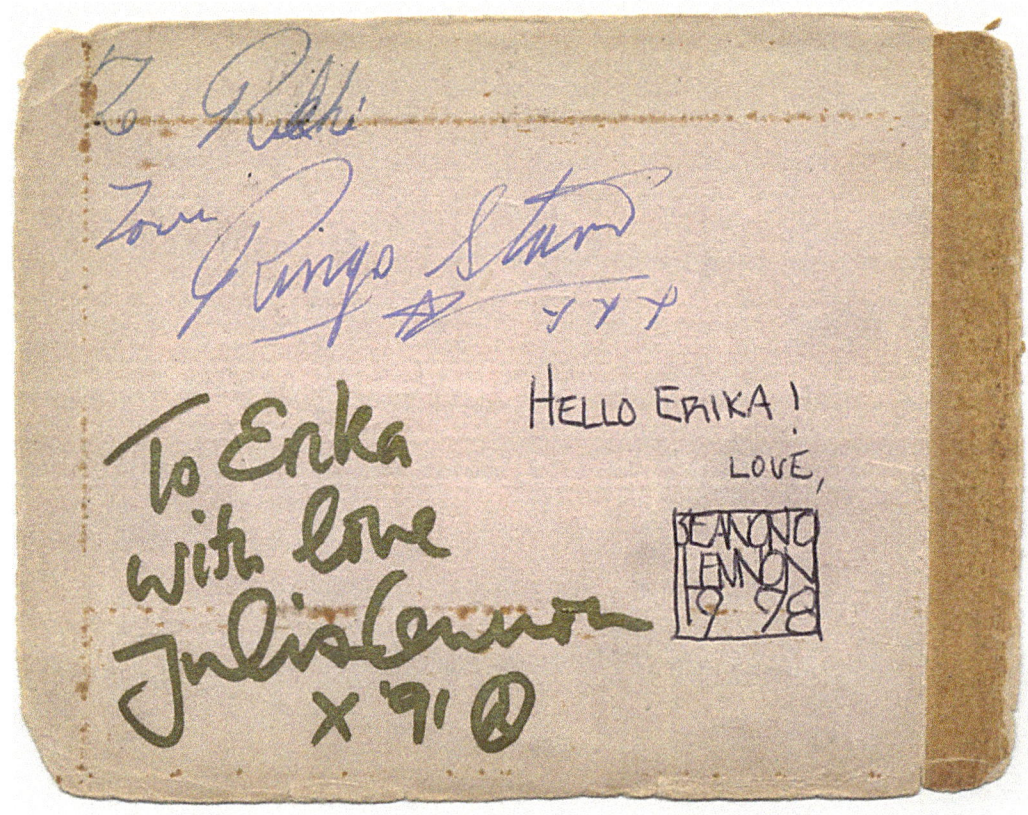

THE BEATLES

Beatles Parlophone card signed by all four on the reverse from late 1962.

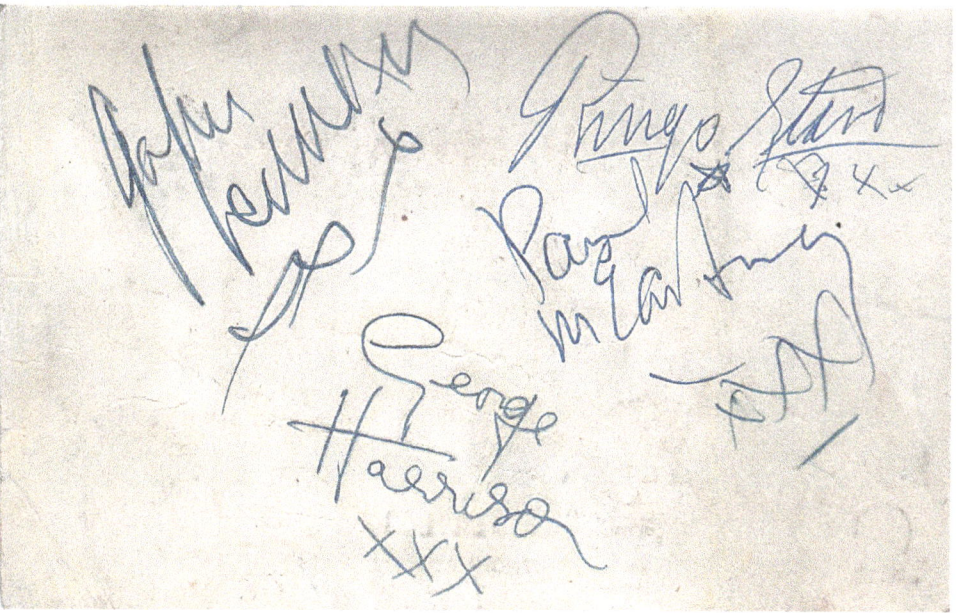

A nice Dezo Hoffman photo of the band performing signed by all four Beatles

THE BEATLES

1963 English poster measuring 17.25 x 22 signed by all four Beatles.

THE BEATLES

The Beatles Show Program signed, incredibly, by all four Beatles.

THE BEATLES

The Beatles concert ticket for Grosvenor signed on the reverse by all four Beatles on May 17, 1963.

My mother, Josie Cliffe was 14 when she went to see the Beatles for the first time. She normally took with her her little autograph book. For some reason she paused and picked up the album cover instead of the record she had been listening to all day. The Beatles were playing at City Hall in Sheffield England in 1963. My mom and grandma went to the show. My mom rushed down to the front to get the Autographs of the fab four. Most of the screaming girls down in front were holding their little autograph books, ones very similar to my moms. She held up the album cover and Paul reached down and took the album all four signed and handed it back to my mother.

Hope you enjoy the album as much as my family has.

Melissa Houser

Please Please Me UK album cover signed on the reverse by all four Beatles, with letter of its history above.

THE BEATLES

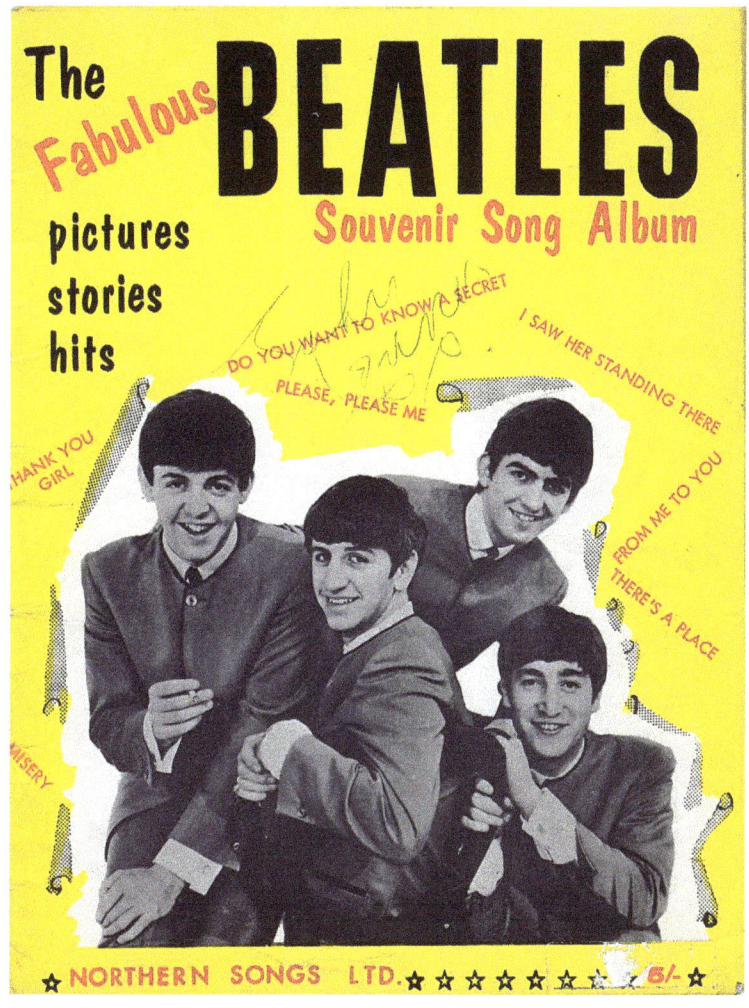

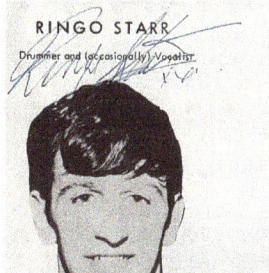

The Beatles Souvenir Song Album booklet signed by John on the front and by Paul, George, and Ringo on their respective bio pages.

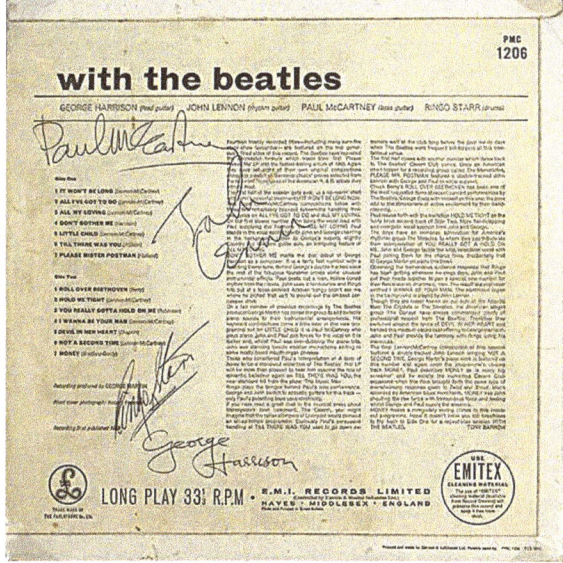
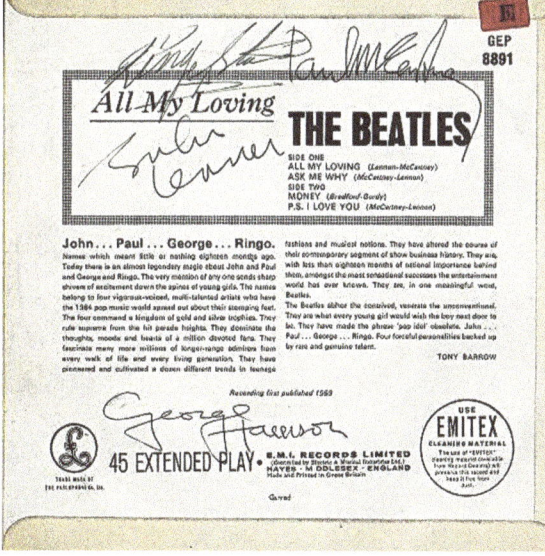

With The Beatles UK album cover signed on the reverse by all four Beatles (left). Extended play UK record cover titled *All My Loving* signed on the reverse by all four Beatles (right).

THE BEATLES

Promotional oversized photo card of The Beatles with signatures by all four on the reverse. Obtained in Sweden in October 1963.

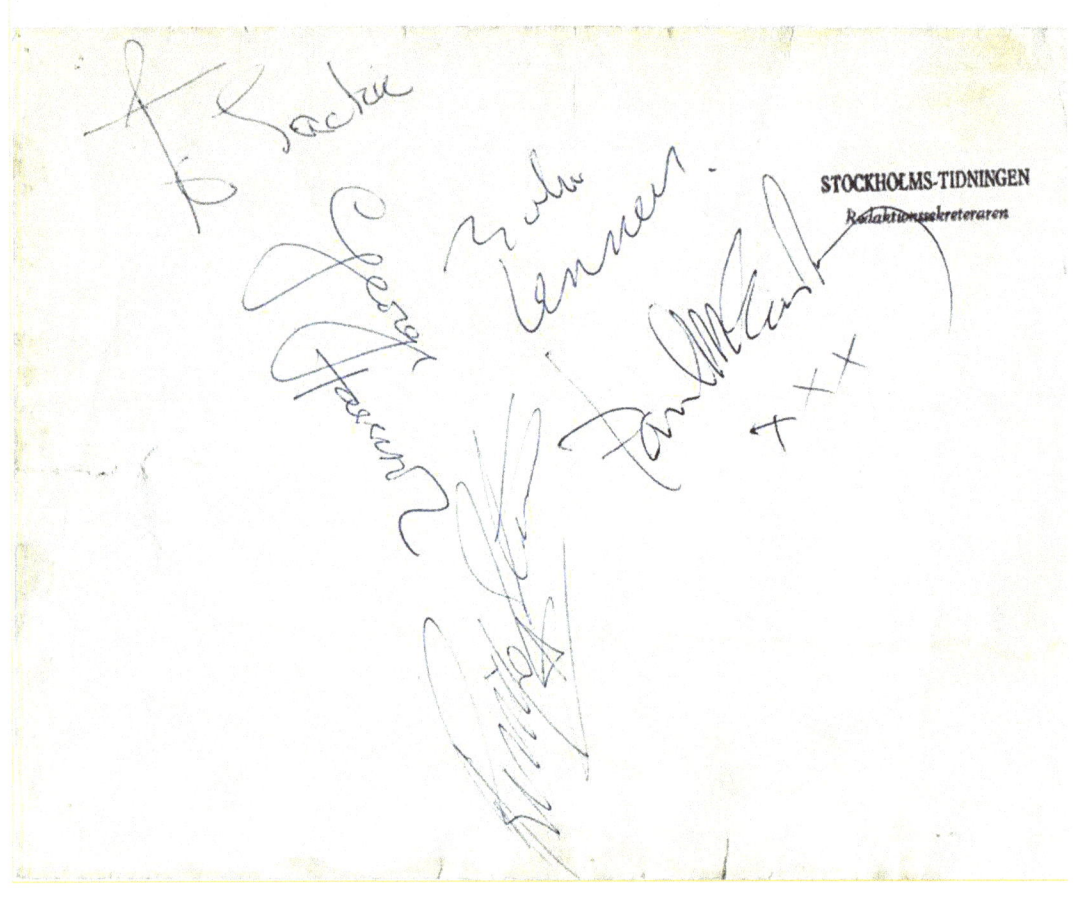

THE BEATLES

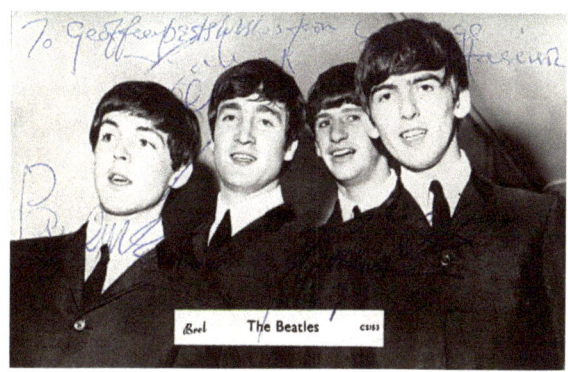

The Beatles Fan Club Card signed on the front by all four Beatles.

The Beatles (Brel) photo card signed with inscription by all four Beatles.

A photo clipping from UK newspaper magazine promoting The Beatles coming to America signed by all four Beatles.

THE BEATLES BY ROYAL COMMAND NOVEMBER 4, 1963

Commemorative Booklet highlighting The Beatles performance from the event.

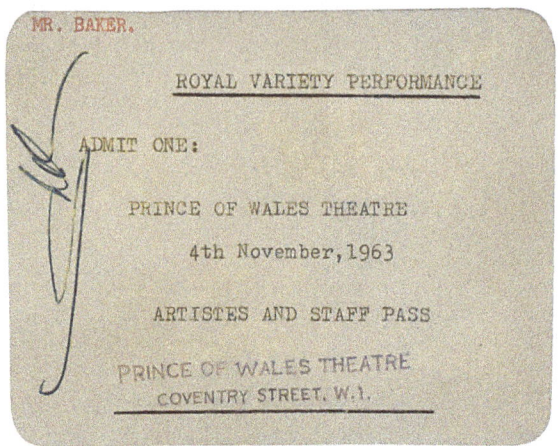

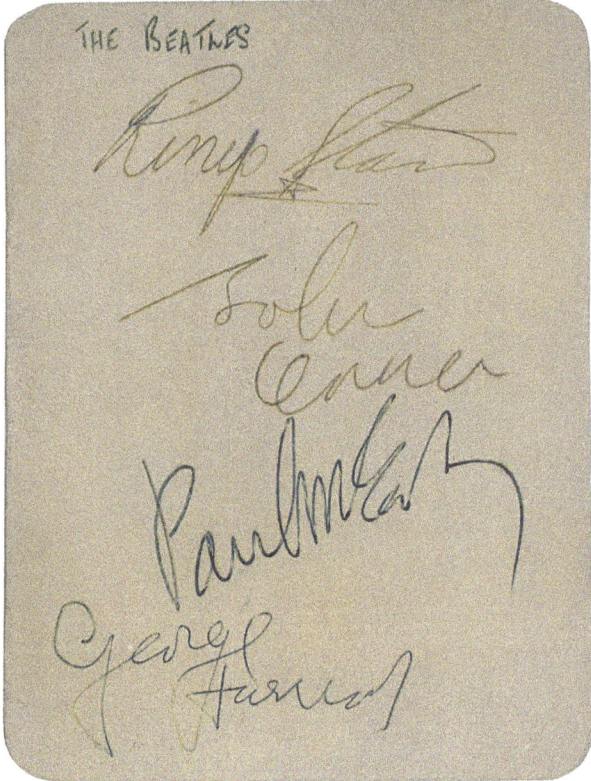

Royal Variety Performance invitation ticket signed by guest performer, Marlene Dietrich and signed by all four Beatles on the reverse.

THE BEATLES BY ROYAL COMMAND NOVEMBER 4, 1963

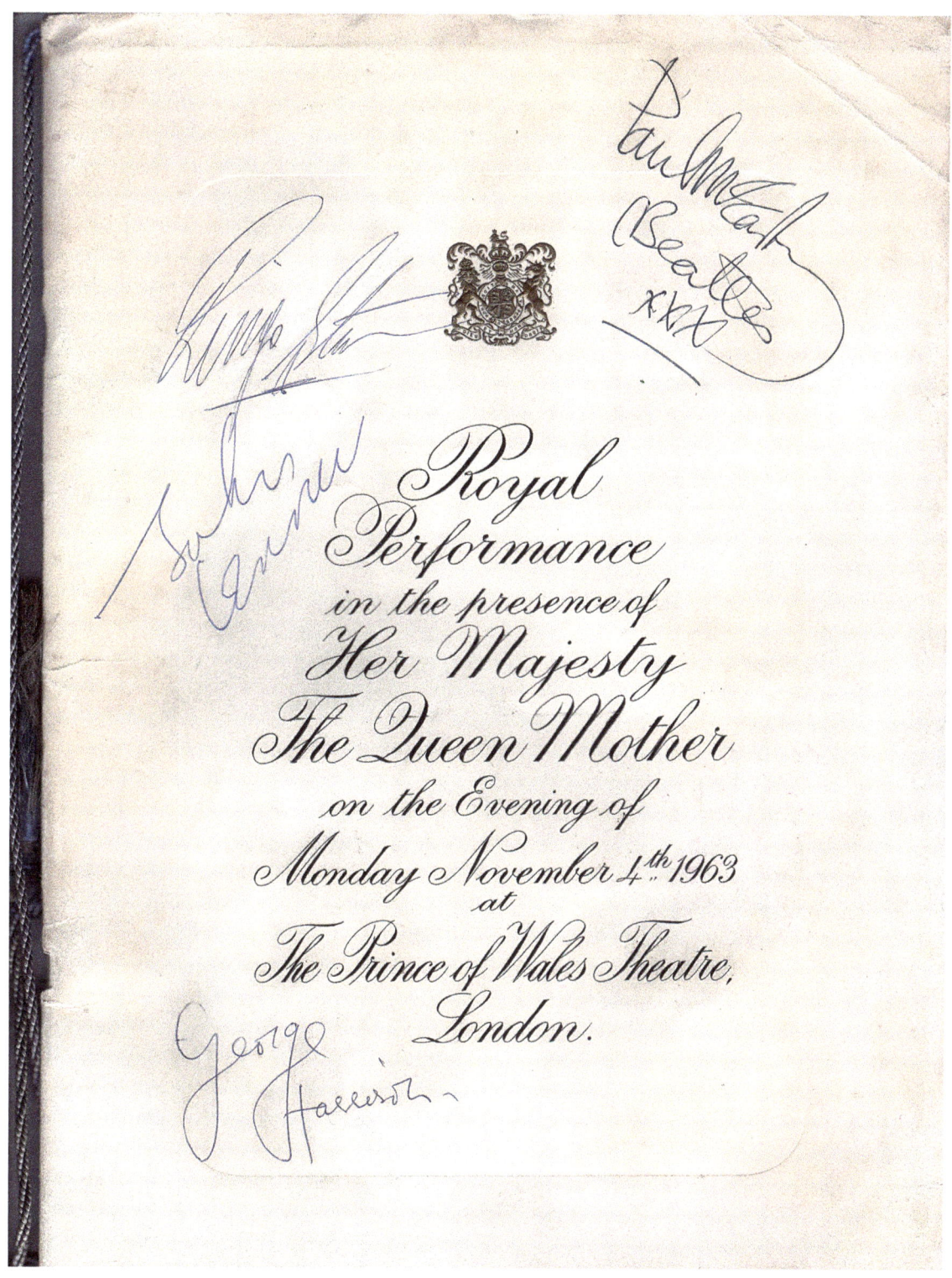

A Royal Command Performance for the Queen Mother program signed by all four Beatles on the front cover. This was the performance when John made the famous remark "Will the people in the cheaper seats clap your hands and the rest of you just rattle your jewelry."

THE BEATLES BY ROYAL COMMAND NOVEMBER 4, 1963

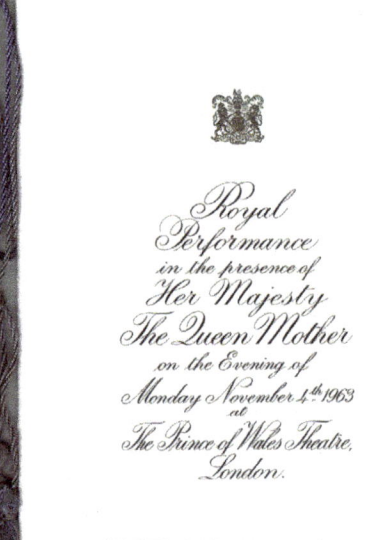
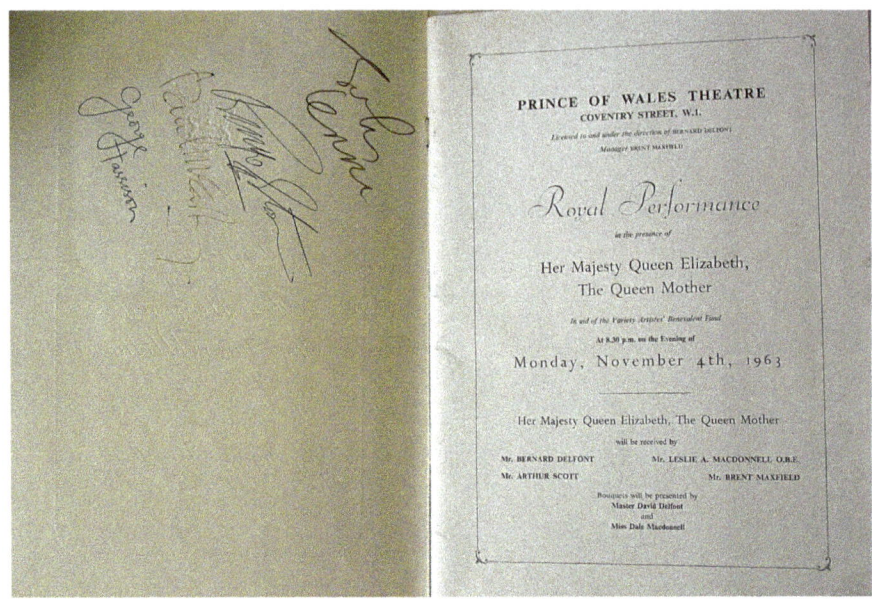

A Royal Command Performance for the Queen Mother program signed by all four Beatles on the inside of the front cover.

THE BEATLES

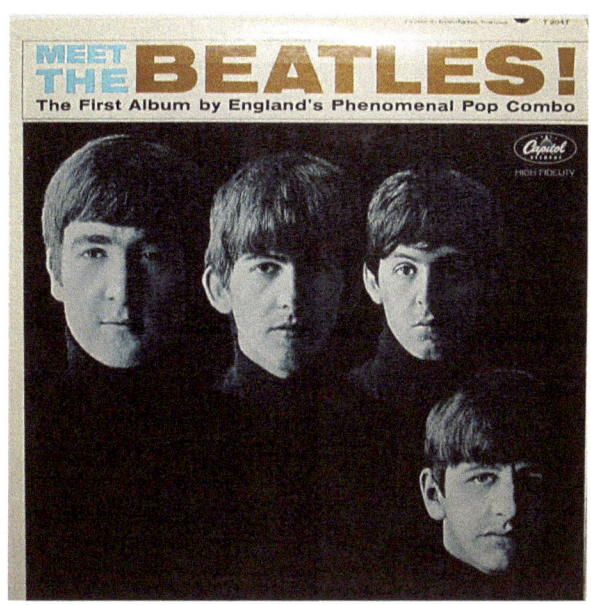

Capitol Records debut album *Meet The Beatles* signed by all four on the reverse on February 9, 1964 with a letter of its history shown below.

The letter reads:

> To Whom It May Concern,
> The record album, Meet the Beatles, was signed for my brother Edward Stein. He worked as a lighting technician at CBS studios in New York City in the late 1950's to 60's. He worked on many shows and events including What's my Line? and The Ed Sullivan Show.
>
> Sincerely,
> Lillian Eisen

A rare promotional Dezo Hoffman photographed 8x10 photo signed by all four Beatles.

▶ 15

THE BEATLES

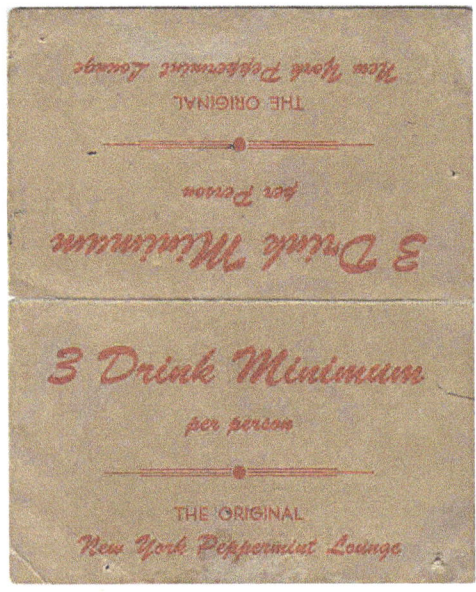
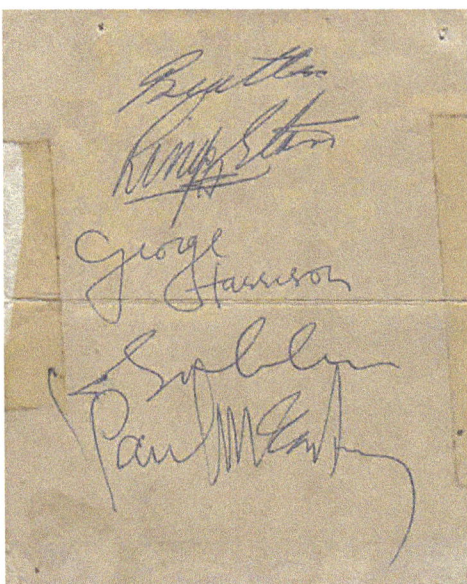

A drink card from the New York Peppermint Lounge in Miami. Inside of card is signed by all four Beatles in February 1964. Manager Brian Epstein gave these signatures to a waitress who was serving them drinks and I obtained them from her.

June 12th, 2006

Attn: Mr. Tom Fontaine

Dear Tom,
The following is the story and history on how I obtained the Beatles autographs.

It was in the year 1964 that the Beatles came to Miami. I was working at the Peppermint Lounge, the hottest nightspot in the Miami Beach area. It was located in North Bay Village, one of the small islands on the causeway leading to the mainland.

The Beatles came in two consecutive nights with their manager Brian Epstein, Feb. 13th and 14th. They did not sit ringside to attract attention to themselves. They sat on the upper level balcony near the rear of the club. Their drink orders was odd--scotch and coke. When I ordered it from the service bartender, he said," Who in hell drinks scotch and coke?"

I waited on them both nights, and the second night I got a little friendlier with Brian. He asked me if I wanted their autographs. I said no but he got them for me anyway and had them sign a Peppermint Lounge minimum drink card.

I have had it in my possession ever since that night until now.

Sincerely,
Shirli Cicirelli

B.- G. "RAMBLERS" with "BEATLES"
At Peppermint Lounge, Miami Beach, Florida

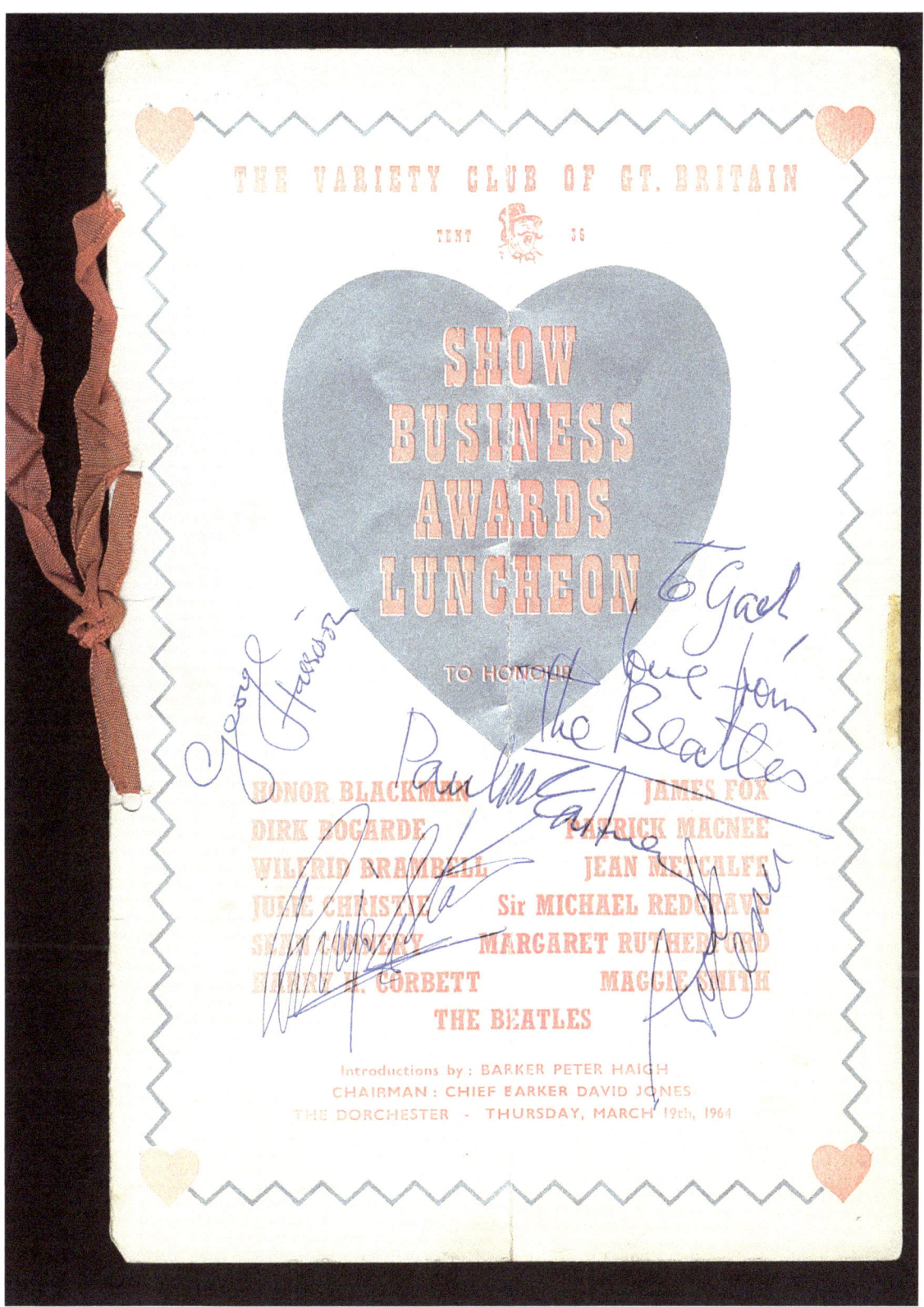

The Variety Club of Great Britain menu signed by all four Beatles on March 19, 1964.

THE BEATLES

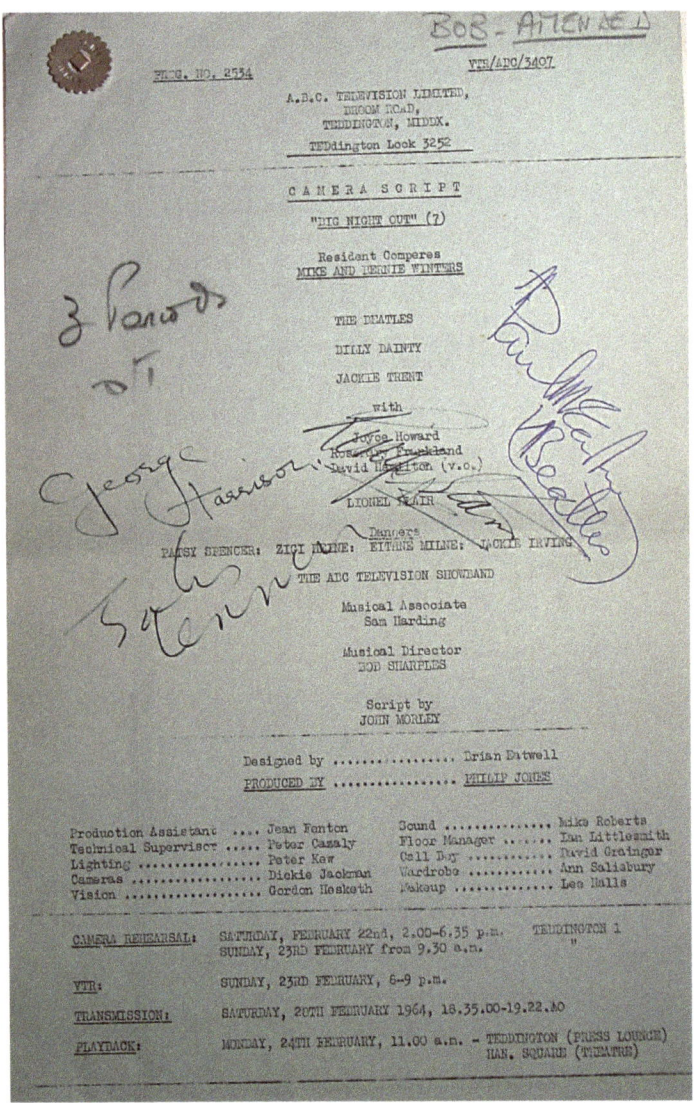

Left, original script for the show Big Night Out, featuring The Beatles, signed on the front by all four. Below: A rare promotional Dezo Hoffman photographed 8x10 photo signed by all four Beatles.

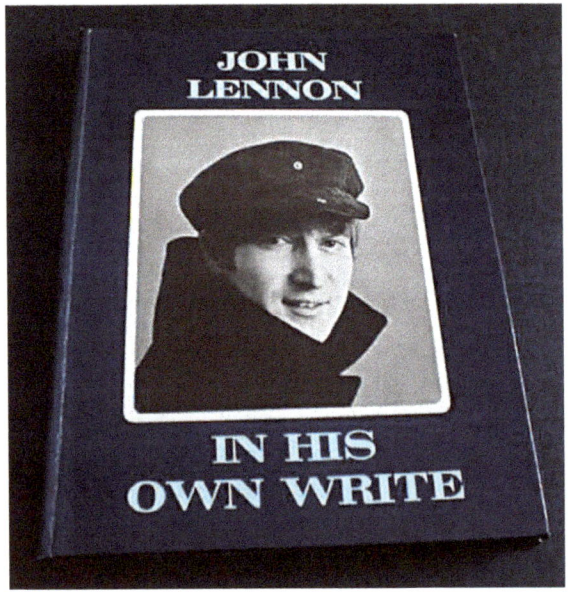

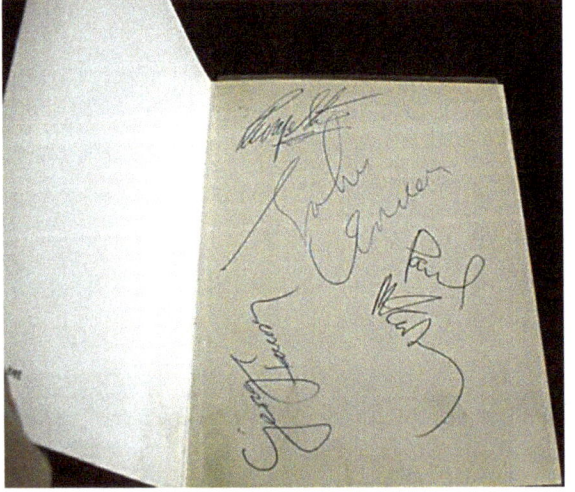

John Lennon's *In His Own Write* book signed on the inside front page by all four Beatles.

THE BEATLES

A Carl Allen Awards invitation ticket signed by all 4 Beatles, their manager Brian Epstein.

> 19

THE BEATLES

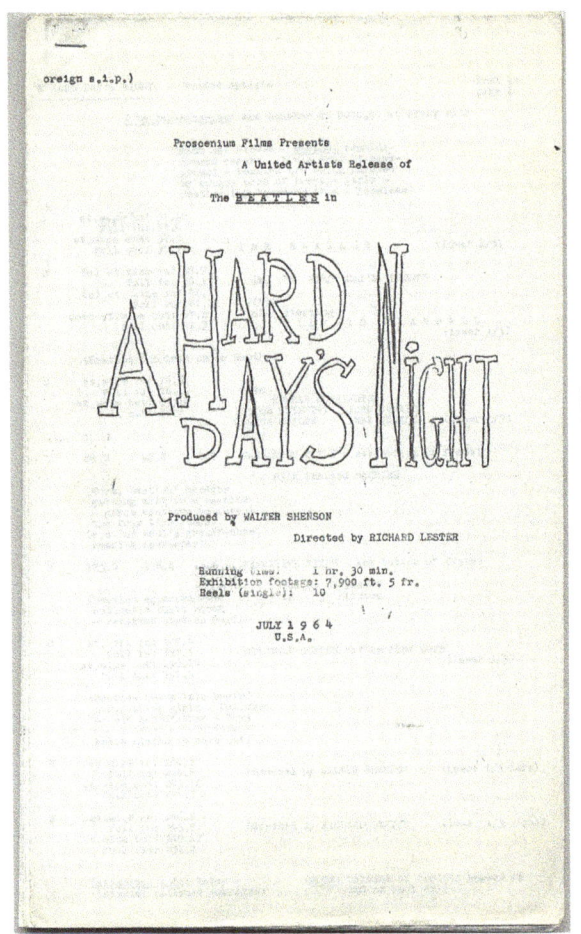

Original Projection Script for The Beatles motion picture *A Hard Day's Night* in 1964.

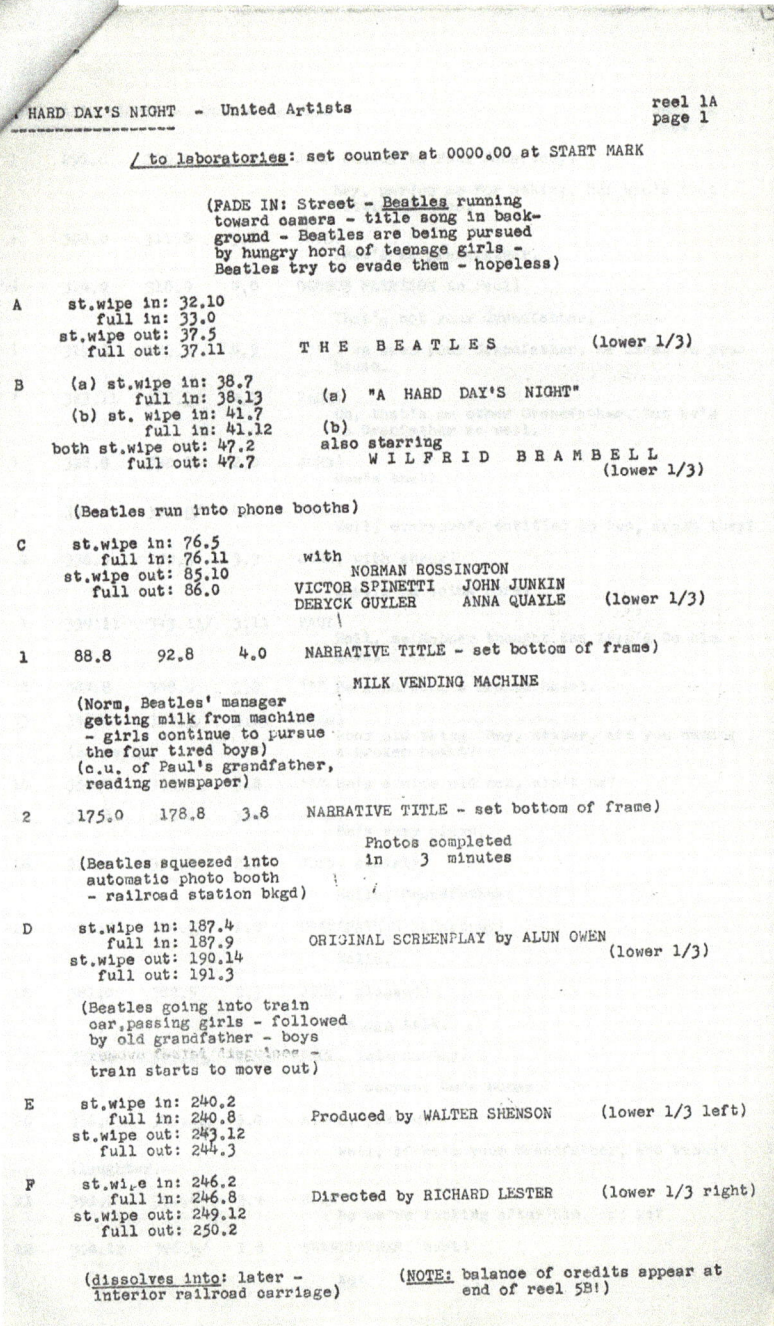

An approximately 12x16 oversized photo picturing all four Beatles and signed by all. What makes this a very cool item is that this photo was taped to the wall on the set of *A Hard Day's Night,* removed and signed during the filming in 1964.

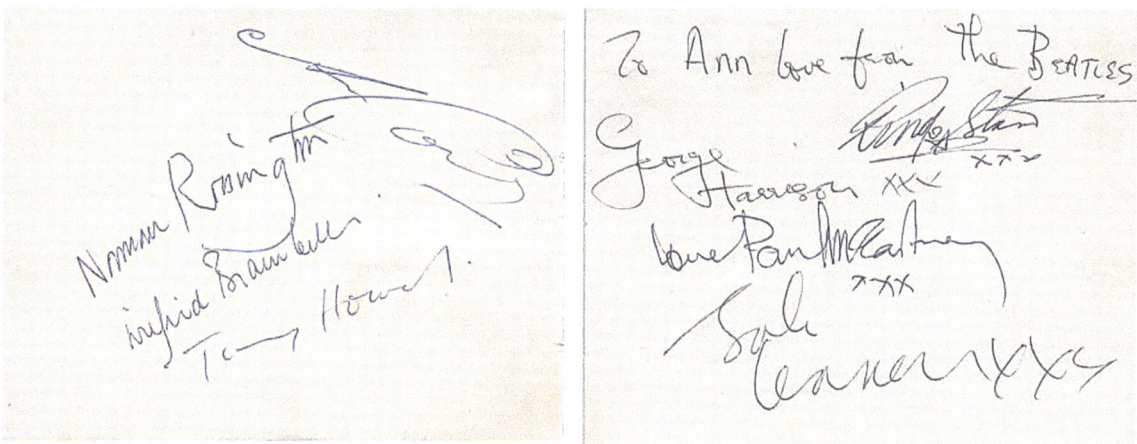

An ensemble of signatures obtained during the filming of *A Hard Day's Night* signed and inscribed nicely by all four Beatles and co-stars from the film in 1964.

A nice set of signatures on the reverse of a train voucher obtained during the filming of *A Hard Day's Night* in 1964 nicely matted with an original photo from the movie.

THE BEATLES

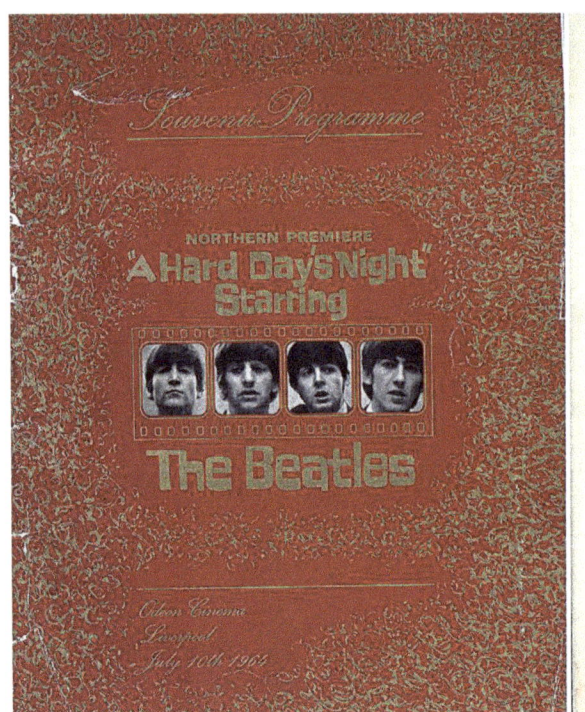

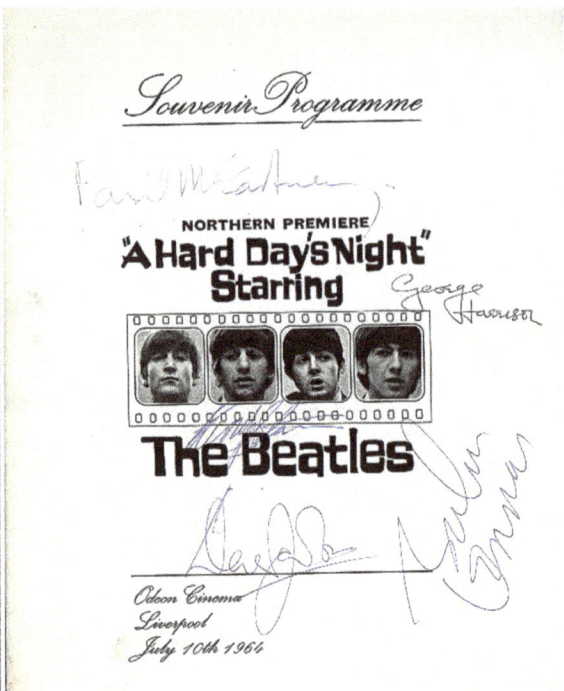

Souvenir program for the Liverpool Premiere of *A Hard Day's Night* signed on the inside page by all four Beatles and personality Derek Jacobs who was on the flight with The Beatles.

A nice set of signatures from 1965 inside a photo folder picturing an early image of The Beatles.

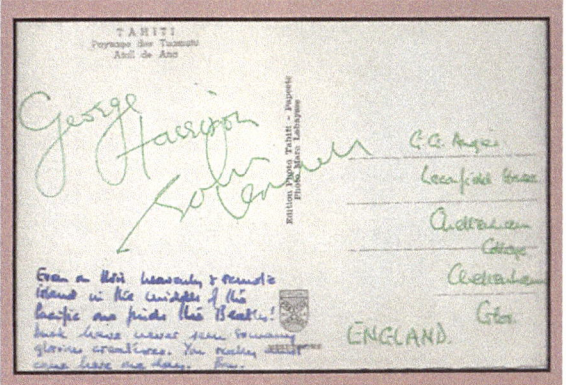

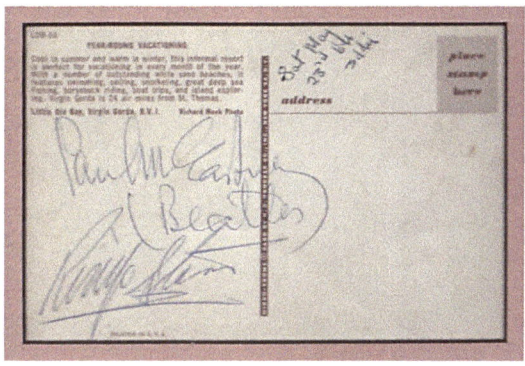

Two postcards autographed by all four Beatles while on holiday. John and George along with Patti Boyd and Cynthia Lennon went on vacation together in Tahiti which is where a lucky fan obtained the signatures. The same for Paul and Ringo who were on holiday together in the Virgin Islands with Maureen Cox and Jane Asher signed a postcard. A rather unique ensemble, catching the Fab 4 vacationing in 1964.

INTRODUCTION

At Woolton village fete I met him. I was a fat schoolboy and, as he leaned an arm on my shoulder, I realised that he was drunk. We were twelve then, but, in spite of his sideboards, we went on to become teenage pals.

Aunt Mimi, who had looked after him since he was so high, used to tell me how he was cleverer than he pretended, and things like that. He had written a poem for the school magazine about a hermit who said: 'as breathing is my life, to stop I dare not dare.' This made me wonder right away - 'Is he deep?' He wore glasses so it was possible, and even without them there was no holding him. 'What 'bus?' he would say to howls of appreciative laughter.

He went to Quarry Bank High School for Boys and later attended to the Liverpool Art College. He left school and played with a group called the Beatles, and, here he is with a book. Again I think - 'Is he deep?' 'Is he arty, with it or cultured?'

There are bound to be thickheads who will wonder why some of it doesn't make sense, and others who will search for hidden meanings.
'What's a Brummer?'
'There's more to 'dubb owld boot' than meets the eye.'
None of it has to make sense and if it seems funny then that's enough.

Paul

P.S. I like the drawings too.

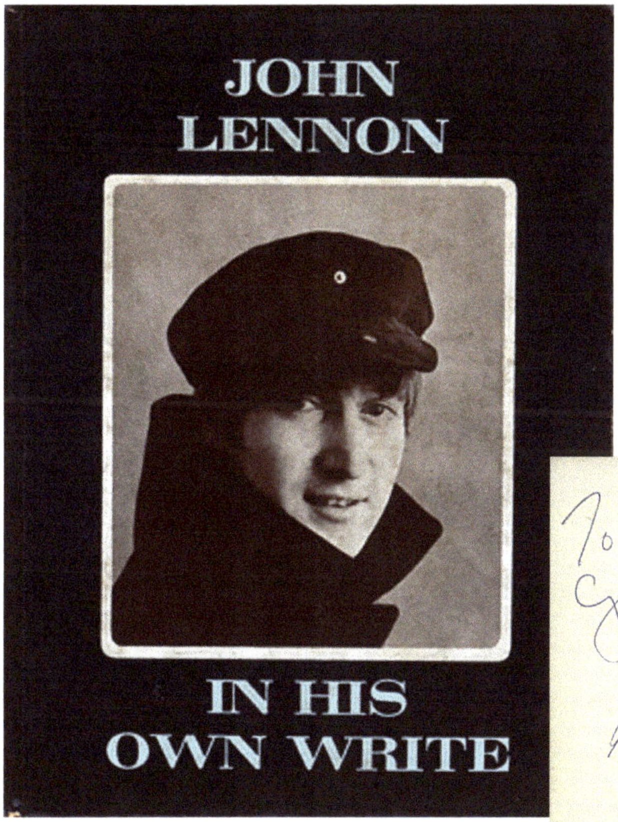

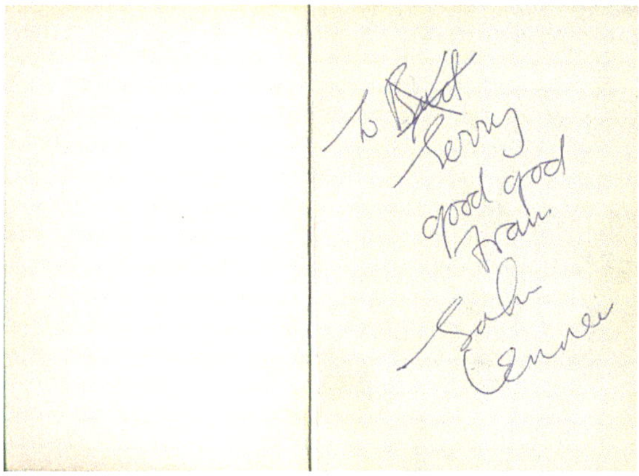

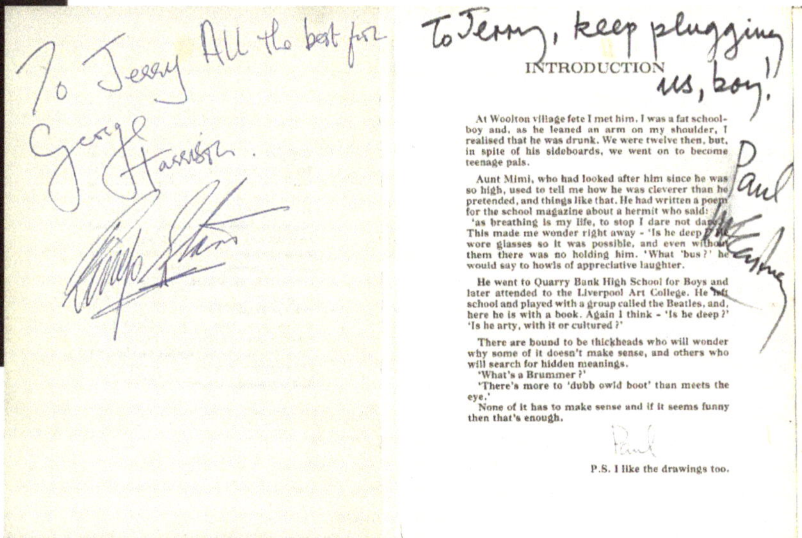

John Lennon's *In His Own Write* book signed on the inside by all four Beatles with annotations.

THE BEATLES

An extremely rare Australian pressing of The Beatles album *Please Please Me* signed by all four Beatles on the reverse in 1964.

Capitalizing on The Beatles craze, a London radio station held a contest to spend the day with The Beatles. The winner, A.F. Prescott, had the Beatles sign the consent form in 1964.

THE BEATLES

A South Pacific *Teal Flight Companion* magazine signed by all four Beatles in flight from their New Zealand tour in 1964.

Proof Advertisement poster that was used for print ads promoting The Beatles latest single, "Can't Buy Me Love," on Capitol Records in 1964.

THE BEATLES

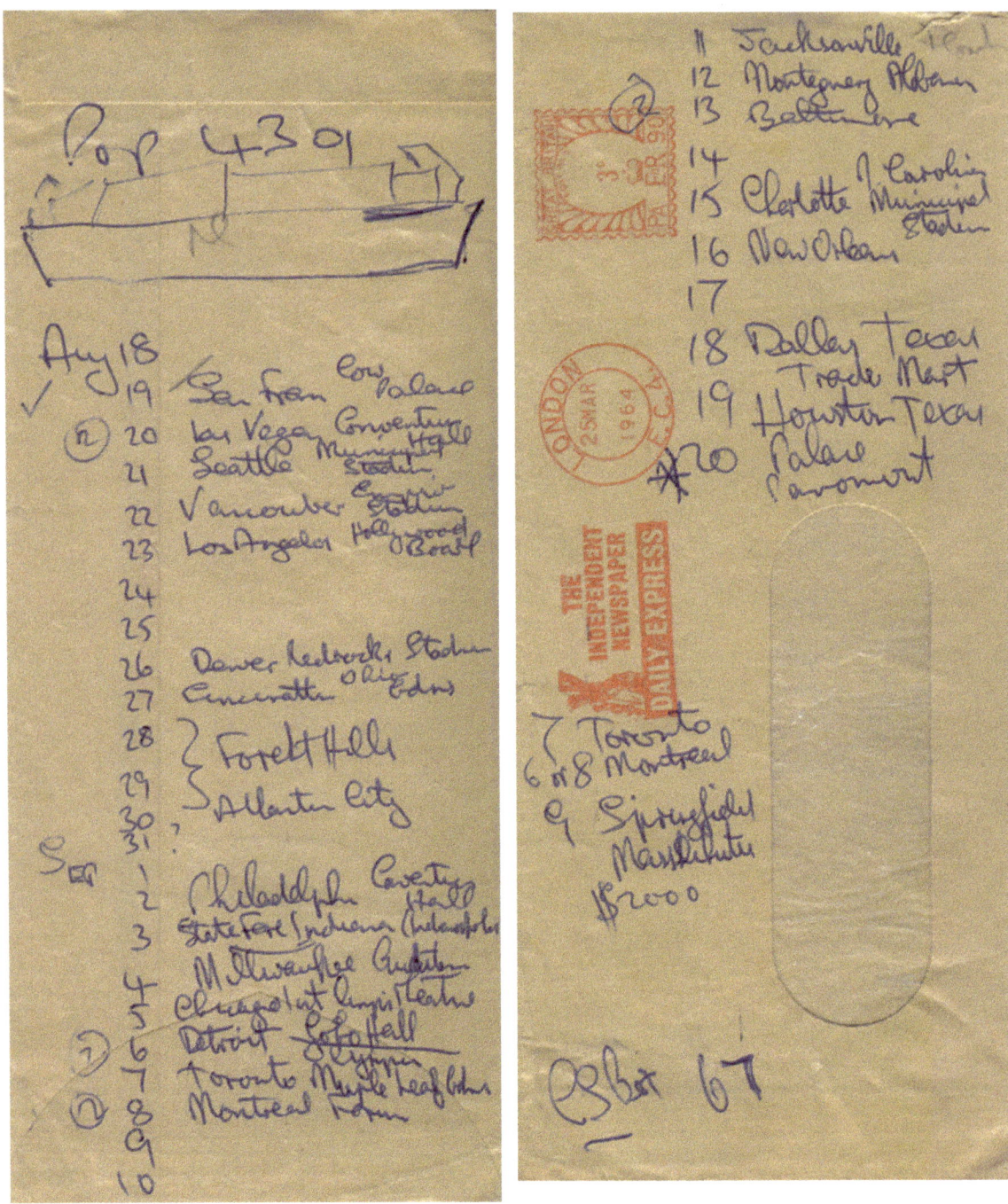

Beatles manger Brian Epstein handwritten itinerary with locations and dates for the Beatles 1964 US tour written on both sides of an envelope.

THE BEATLES

A 1964 US Summer Tour program signed on the inside first page by all four Beatles.

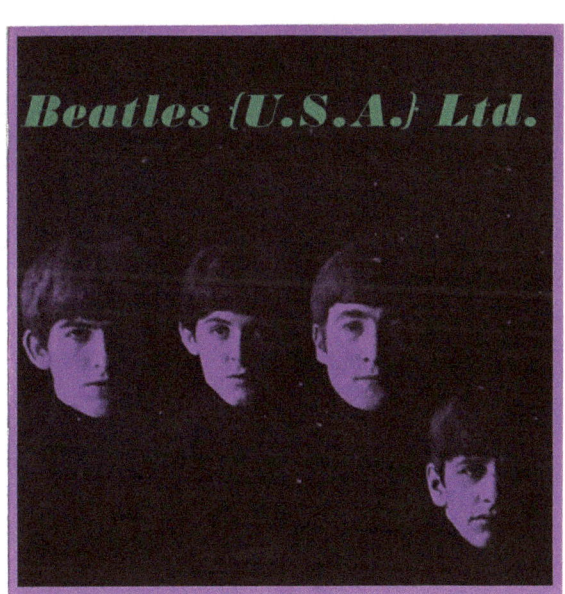

THE BEATLES

RIAA sales Gold record award presented to The Beatles for the song, "I Feel Fine," in 1964.

THE BEATLES

A Best Wishes card from The Beatles to fan club Secretary Ann Collinham signed by all four. Not sure why George wrote to Mary, possibly that was her real name. It is a little tongue and cheek however as Paul wrote Collingham for his last name. It was all good fun.

Original script for the Beatles second movie, *Help!* Since there was no title at the time, they gave it a working title of *Beatles 2*.

THE BEATLES

Beatles *Bahamas Special* menu. This is a larger and more elaborate menu signed on the reverse by all four Beatles and co-star Elenor Bron. It was obtained during a flight to or from the Bahamas when they were filming their film, *Help!* in 1965.

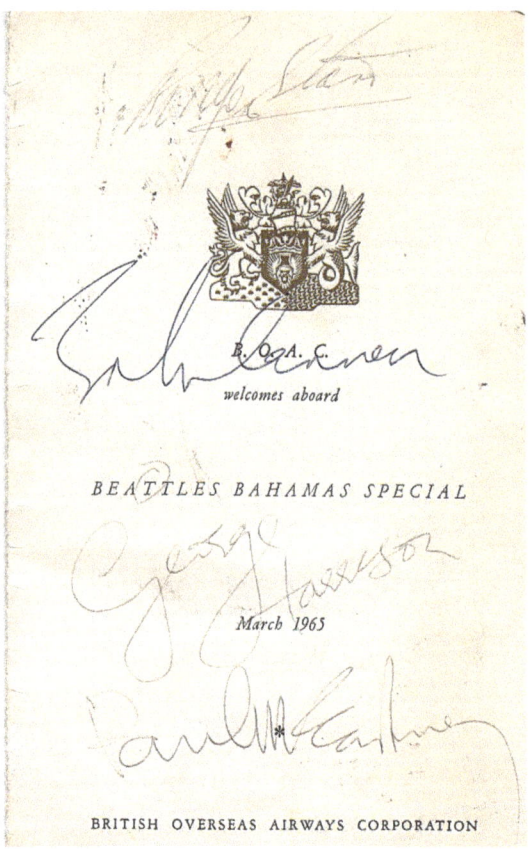

Beatles *Bahamas Special* menu signed during flight to the Bahamas when they were filming their film, *Help!* in 1965. Notice on this particular menu the Beattles spelling.

Above: an 8 x 10 photo of the Beatles in the Bahamas, signed by all four and director of the film, Richard Lester. From their movie *Help!* in 1965.

At right, an alternate 8x10 photo of The Beatles in the Bahamas signed by all Paul, George, and Ringo in 1965. From their movie, *Help!*

THE BEATLES

An autograph book containing the signatures of The Beatles, their wives, girlfriends, manager and co stars from their move *Help!* Signed in 1965.

THE BEATLES

Victor Spinetti's fur hat worn during the Austrian winter scenes in the movie *Help!*

THE BEATLES

A Royal World Premiere program for the movie *Help!* at the London Pavilion on July 29, 1965. Signed on the reverse by all four Beatles and Beatles producer George Martin and his wife, Judy.

THE BEATLES

A large set of photos on backer board measuring 20 x 30 featuring The Beatles from the movie *Help!* It is the only set I have ever encountered that leads me to believe they possibly were used as a display, promoting the movie.

THE BEATLES

A nice set of signatures obtained at the 1965 Poll winners Concert held at Wembley Arena in England, accompanied by the original ticket and press photo from the event.

THE BEATLES

A Pan Am postcard from France signed nicely by all four Beatles on the reverse in 1965.

A unique Capitol Records promotional 8x10 double image photo, signed twice at various times by Lennon, McCartney, and Starr. The autographs were obtained in the 1970s in New York. From the Howard Siegel Collection.

THE BEATLES

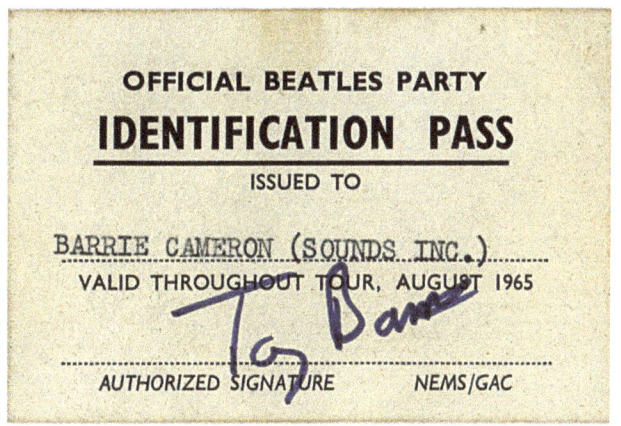

Tony Barrow's official crew press ID card for their August 1965 US tour. Barrow was The Beatles press officer.

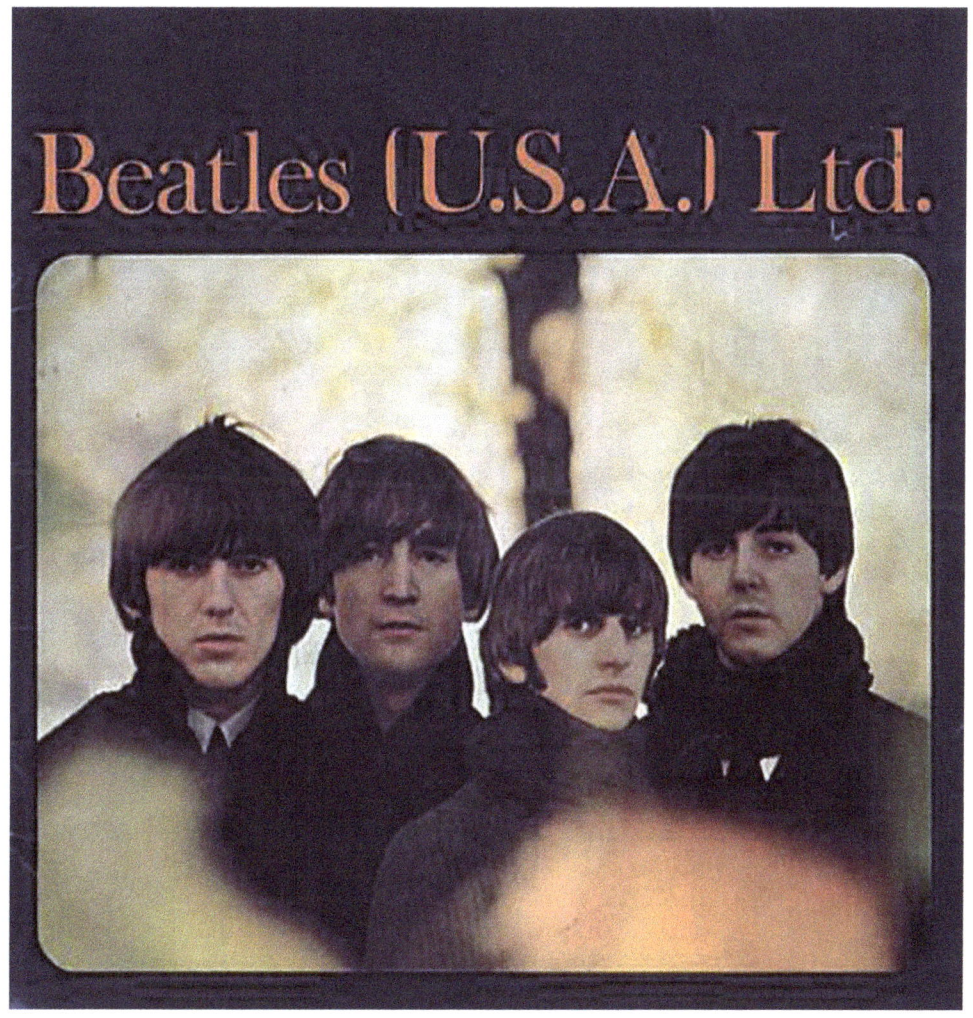

THE BEATLES

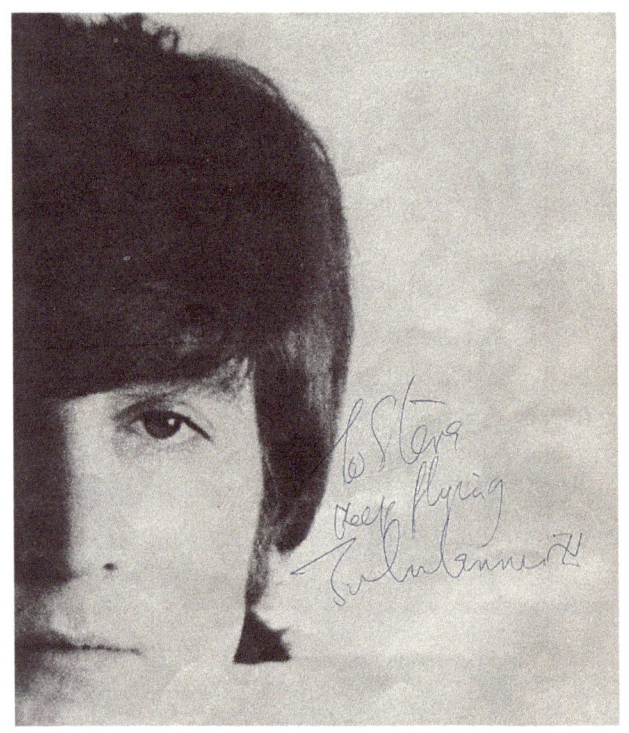

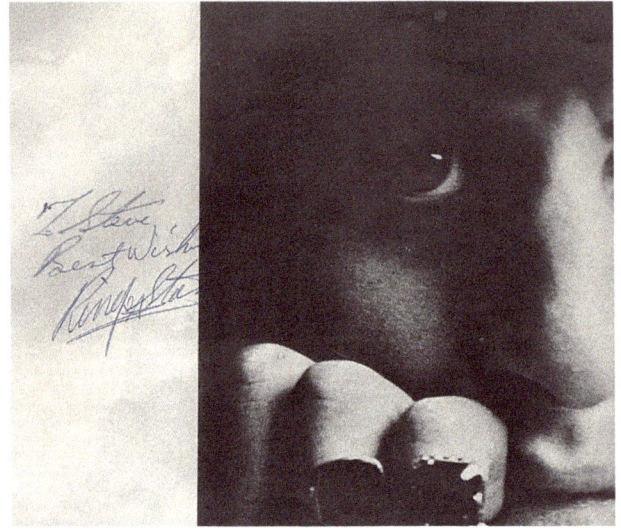

A 1965 Beatles US Tour program, signed inside with inscriptions by all four Beatles This was signed to Steve, a Discotech Dancer in one of the opening acts for the tour.

THE BEATLES

Beatles signed photo on a hot August night in Los Angeles when The Beatles met their idol, Elvis Presley. This photo was signed to Elvis's cousin, Billy Smith, with documentation from Billy.

IN 1965 THE BEATLES CAME TO CALIFORNIA. WHILE THEY WERE THERE THEY VISITED ELVIS AT HIS HOME AT 525 PERUGIA WAY BEL AIR. I, MY WIFE JO, AND OUR SON DANNY LIVED WITH ELVIS AT HIS HOME. WE WERE FORTUNATE TO MEET AND TALK WITH EACH OF THEM. ALSO WE WERE ABLE TO OBTAIN THREE AUTOGRAPHS FROM EACH ONE OF THEM. I OBTAINED TWO AUTOGRAPHED PICTURES.

BILLY SMITH
Billy Smith

THE BEATLES

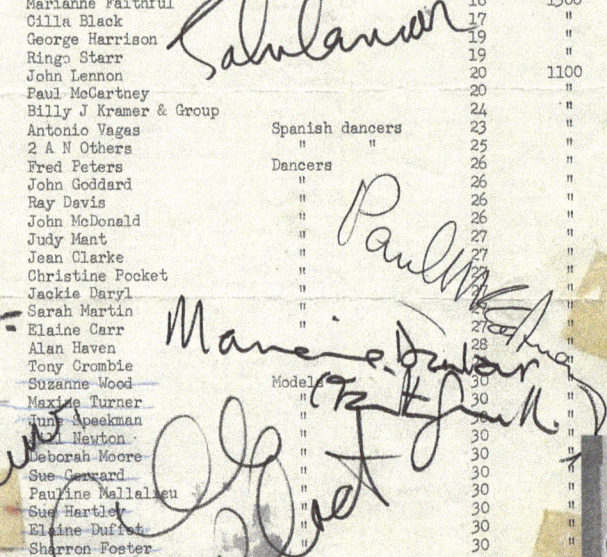

The Music of Lennon and McCartney call sheet for the 1965 TV special. It is signed by John and Paul as well as other artists who appeared on the special — including Marianne Dunbar (Faithfull) and Cilla Black. November 2, 1965.

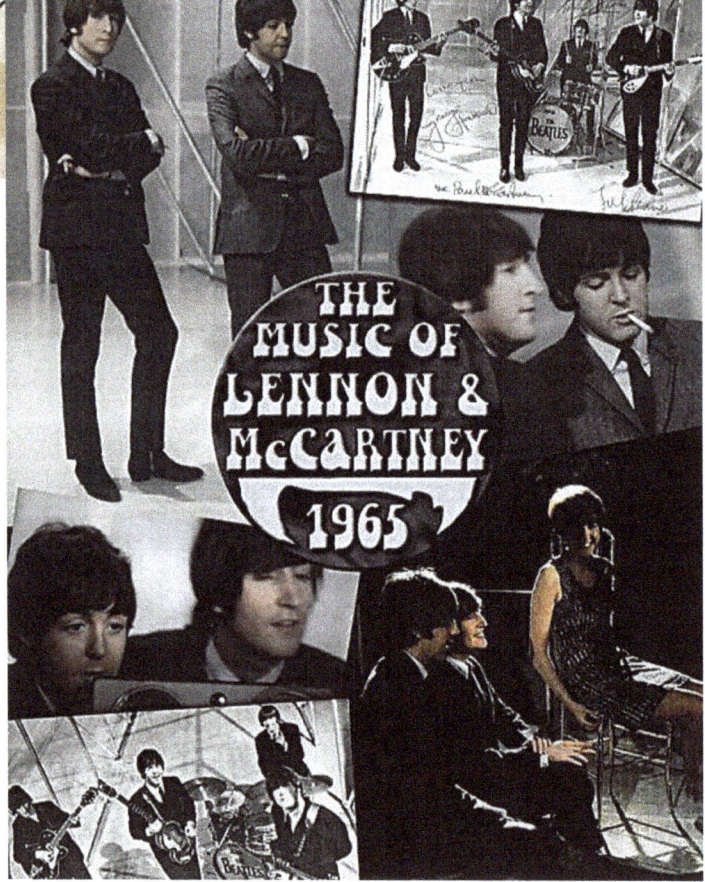

THE BEATLES

A Kuwait Airlines sticker patch with the peel off signed by all four Beatles. Obtained on the plane during their trip to Manila. The Beatles concert ticket from July 4, 1966 in Manila, Philippines. One of the most rare tickets to survive and to surface.

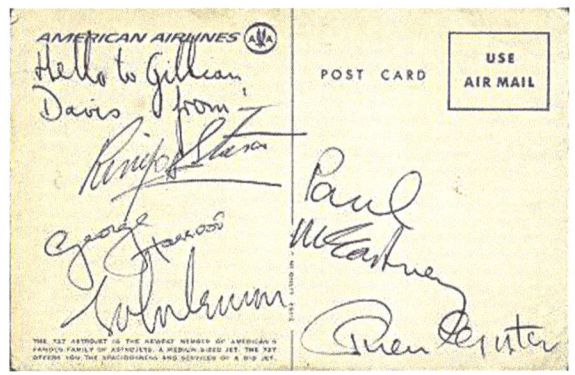

An American Airlines postcard signed by all four Beatles and manager Brian Epstein in August 1966.

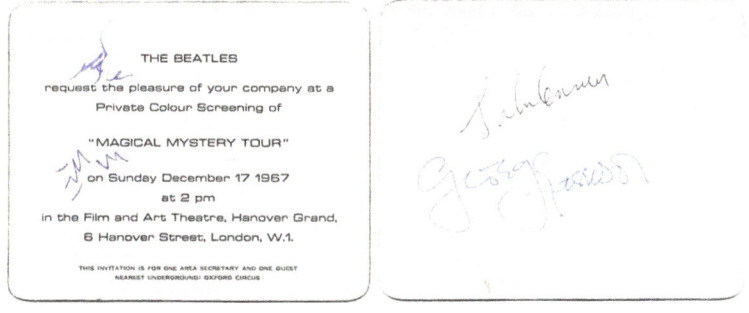

Invitation card from The Beatles to attend a private screening of the Beatles movie *The Magical Mystery Tour* in London on December 17, 1967 signed on the reverse by John Lennon and George Harrison.

English postcard signed on the reverse by John Lennon and George Harrison from the reception for the private screening of *The Magical Mystery Tour*.

➤ 41

THE BEATLES

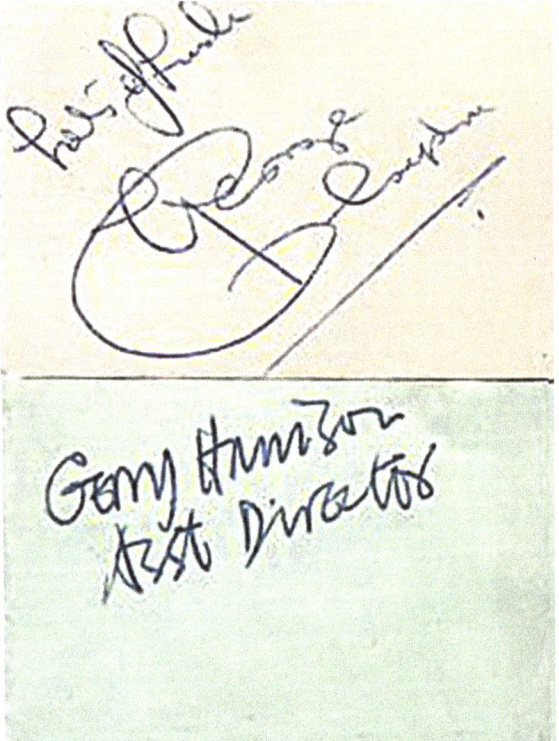

A 1967 Beatles fan club card signed by all four Beatles on the reverse. Signatures were obtained during the filming of Magical Mystery Tour. Additional signatures associated with the film were also obtained.

THE BEATLES

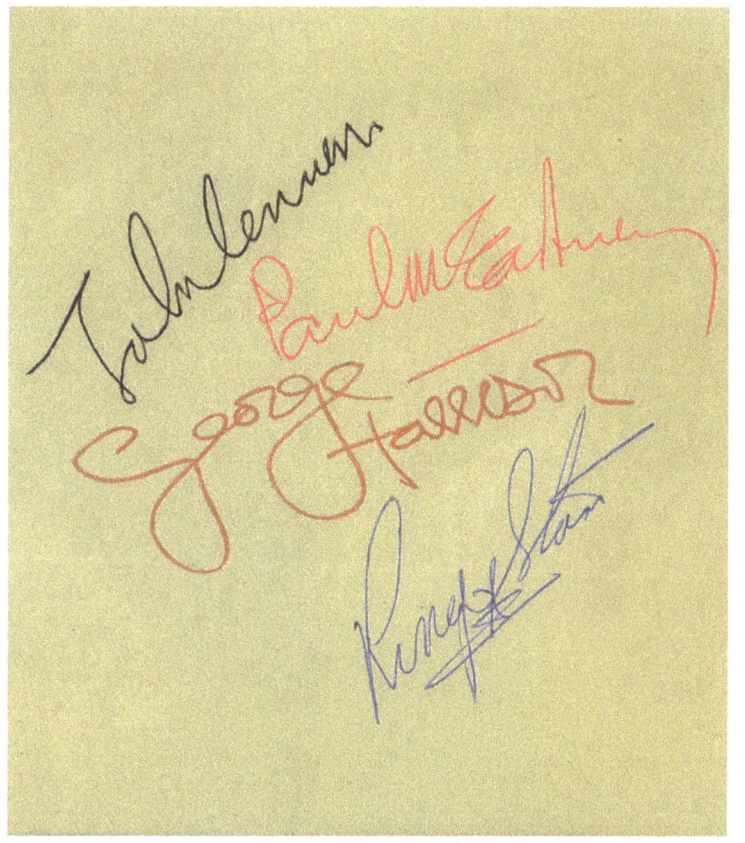 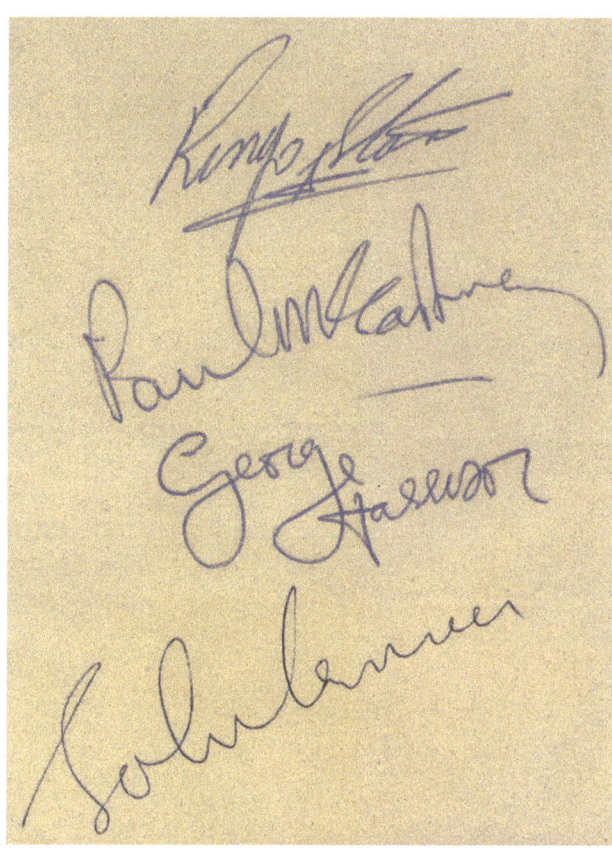

Nice sets of signatures by all four Beatles obtained in 1967 during the filming of Magical Mystery Tour.

 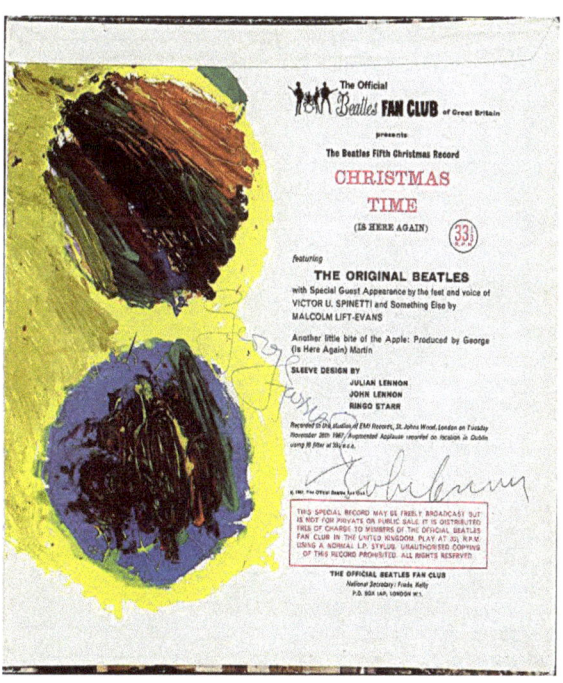

Beatles Christmas message to the fan club flexi disc signed on the reverse by John Lennon and George Harrison. Signatures were obtained during the private screening and reception for *The Magical Mystery Tour.*

➤ 43

THE BEATLES

A set of signatures of all four Beatles from a fan's autograph book. Signatures were obtained in Rishikesh when they attended lectures by the Maharishi Mahesh Yogi in 1968. Accompanied by a letter from the recipient's family member.

To Whom It May Concern

Re: Beatles Memorabilia

My Mother's employer was preparing to depart for India with the Brighton Transcendental Meditation Centre to the Maharashi Mahesh Yogi Centre. My Mother mentioned that I was still lamenting that I hadn't managed to obtain a whole set of signatures and her employer offered to take my autograph book with her just in case she was more successful. She managed to return with the 4 autographs together with two strands of John's hair as a gift for me.

I have kept these mementoes these past 35 years in a childhood memory box before deciding to sell them knowing that I will always have the memory and they will, no doubt, afford much pleasure to the recipient.

Yours faithfully

THE BEATLES

A set of original art cels of all four Beatles' characters from their film *Yellow Submarine* in 1968.

MACLEN Music Ltd. change of secretary document from 1969, signed by John Lennon, Paul McCartney and future Apple president, Neil Aspinall.

➤ 45

THE BEATLES

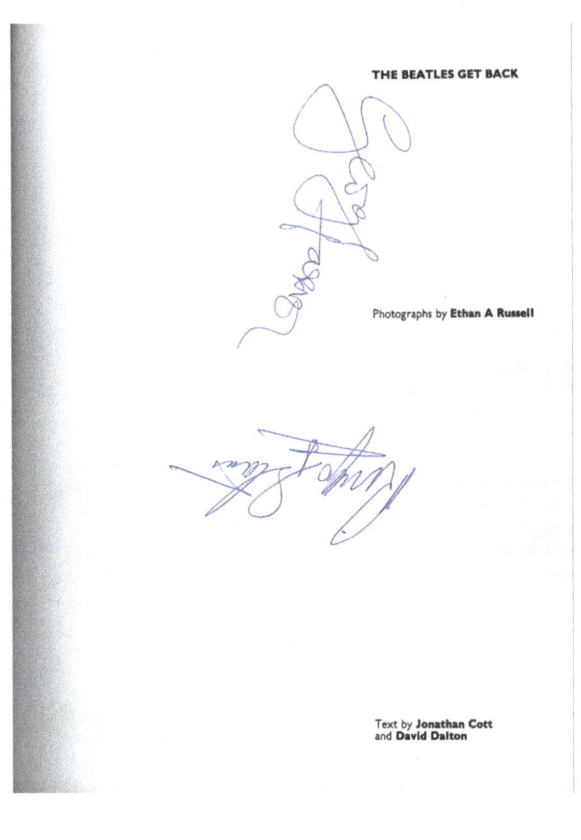

A rare *Get Back* book signed on the inside by George Harrison and Ringo Starr. These signatures were obtained right before the Beatles break up in April 1970, and are quite rare.

Original unpublished 8x10 photos of The Beatles at their press conference in Cincinnati, Ohio in 1964. The photo was signed by all four members at various times in the 1970s, after their breakup.

JOHN LENNON

Small picture of John cut out from a group picture signed on the reverse with the date and location (The Cavern).

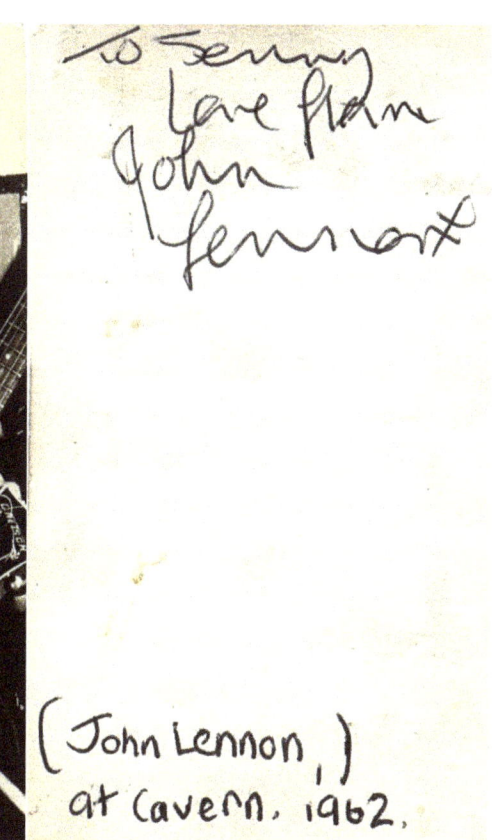

John Lennon Promo Card signed nicely by John in 1962 on the reverse with inscription "Best Wishes" in German.

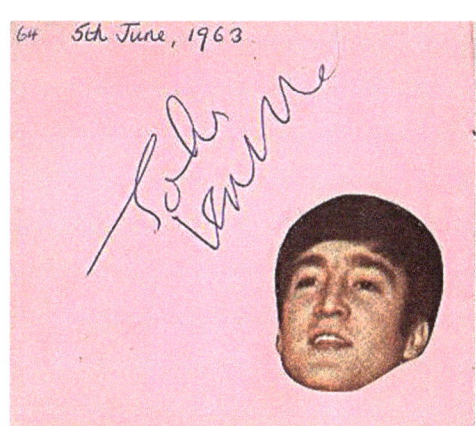

An autograph page by John on June 5, 1963.

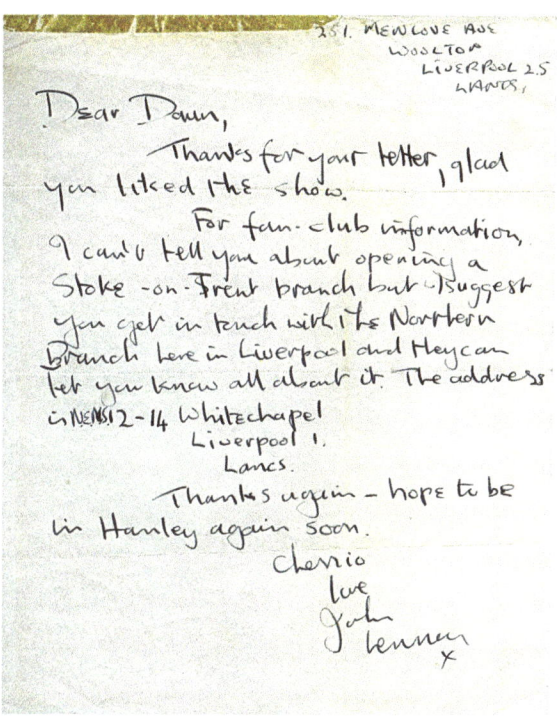

Handwritten letter to a fan from John Lennon, sent from his Menlove Avenue address in 1962.

JOHN LENNON

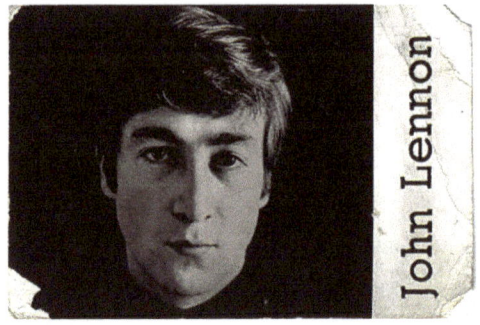

John Lennon Promo Card signed with inscription on the reverse from 1962.

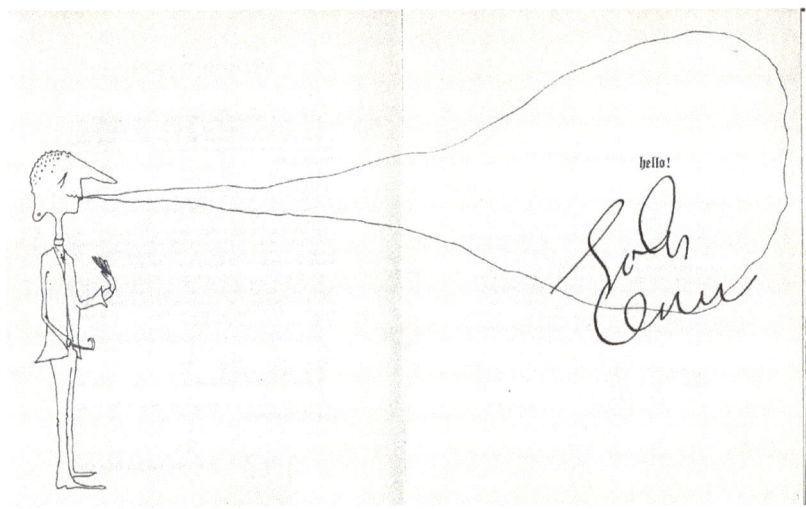

John Lennon's book *In His Own Write* signed by John on one of his drawings contained in the book from 1964.

A nice picture folder featuring a candid photo of John and signed nicely with dedication on the opposite side, from 1964.

JOHN LENNON

A candid photograph of Ringo, filming a scene for *A Hard Day's Night*. Signed on the reverse by John Lennon in 1964.

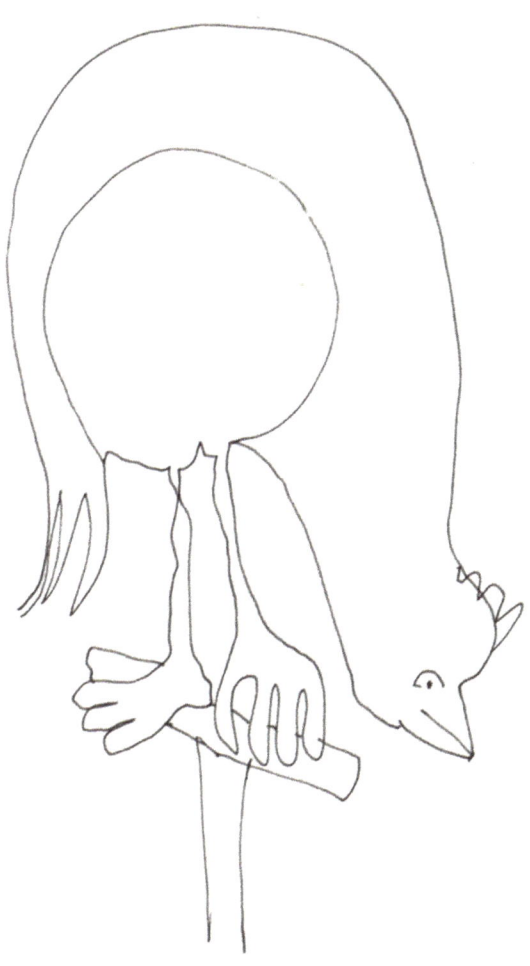

Original hand drawn sketch of a bird on a perch by John Lennon, similar to drawings from his book *In His Own Write*.

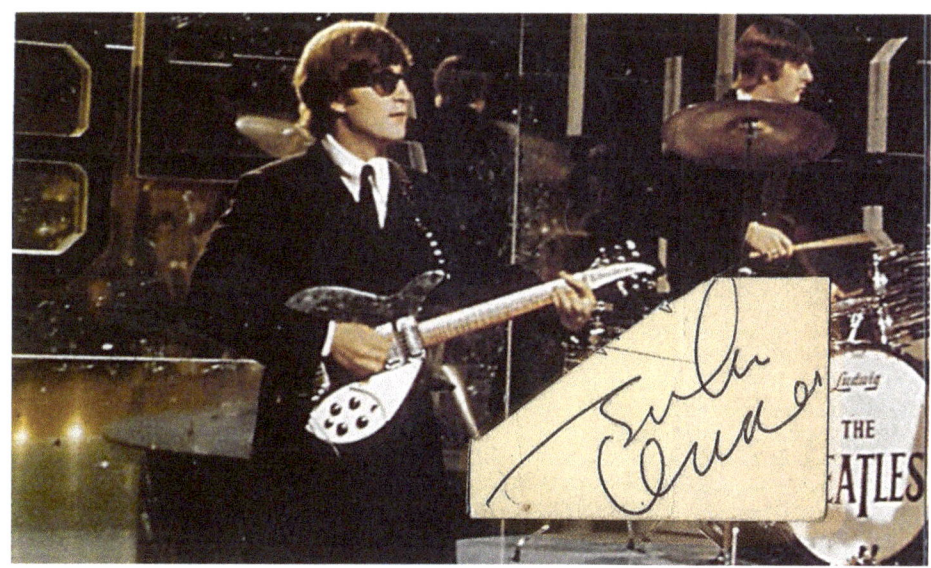

A color photo magazine page of John with a clipped 1964 signature attached.

JOHN LENNON

COPYRIGHT PHOTO
Dezo Hoffmann Ltd.
39 WARDOUR STREET   01-437-8441
LONDON W1V 3HA

Original Dezo Hoffman photos with his stamp on the reverse, picturing John and Cynthia Lennon in Miami in February 1964.

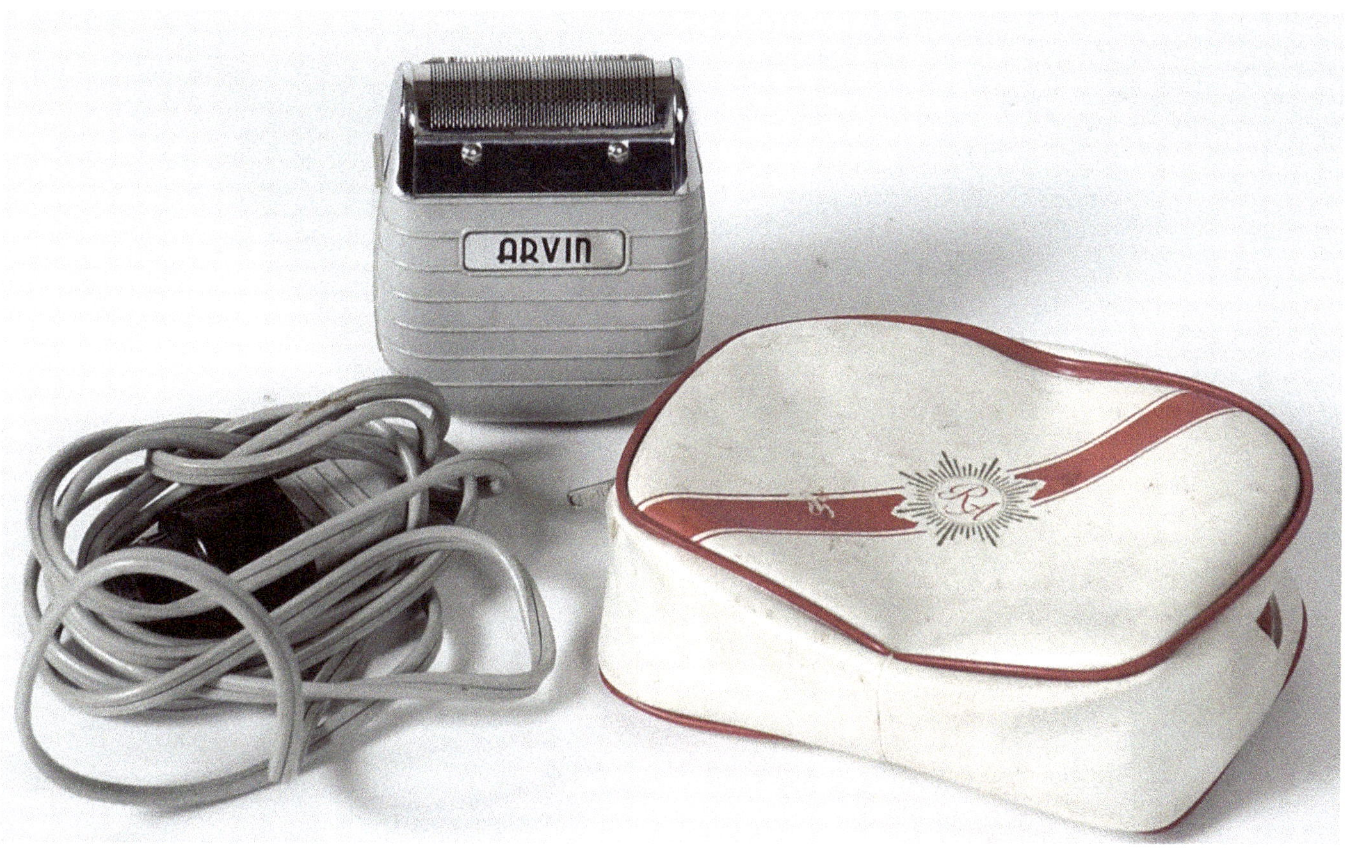

John Lennon's personally owned travel razor with case, used during The Beatles tour years. This came from John's housekeeper, Dot Jarlett. John gave many items to Dot over the years. She was employed by the Lennons in the 1960s.

John Lennon wrote a second book titled *A Spaniard in the Works,* released in 1965. John has signed on the inside cover page.

JOHN LENNON

Eastman Kodak Co instamatic movie camera bought by John and used by him on many occasions at our home "Kenwood" in Weybridge

Cynthia Lennon.

588A

CHRISTIES

John Lennon's personally owned and used movie camera from the 1960s. A note from Cynthia Lennon accompanies, verifying its provenience.

A picture of John from *Beatles Monthly* magazine, signed on his image in 1965.

JOHN LENNON

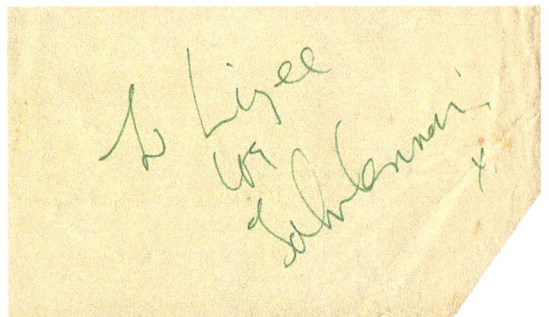

Apple Scruff girl Lizzie Bravo met with The Beatles and received their autographs on many occasions. This one is a nicely signed signature on a page dedicated to Lizzie from her collection. A magazine photo of John and Cynthia Lennon, signed by John, is also from her collection.

A candid photograph of John at his home, signed by John on the front, lightly, and boldly on the reverse in 1967.

A *Magical Mystery Tour* EP signed by John Lennon in the centerfold from 1967.

JOHN LENNON

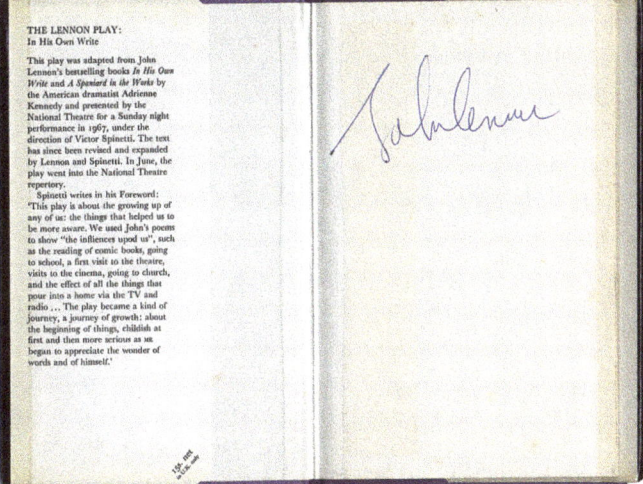

The Lennon play, In His Own Write, by John Lennon and Victor Spinetti signed on the inside by Lennon in 1968. This is the only signed copy of the first edition that has surfaced to date. The unsigned book is also quite rare to obtain.

Publishing agreement from 1968 regarding the Beatles' song "Sexy Sadie" signed on the revere by John Lennon and Neil Aspinall on behalf of MACLEN MUSIC.

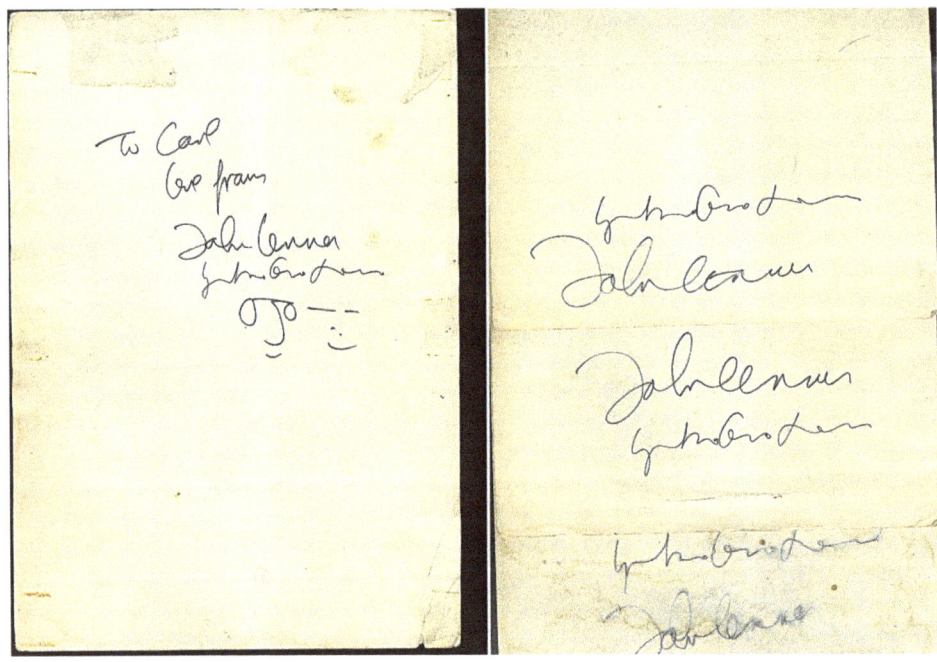

A set of pictures of each Beatle signed on the reverse with dedication on John's photo by John Lennon and Yoko Ono, taken from *The White Album*.

JOHN LENNON

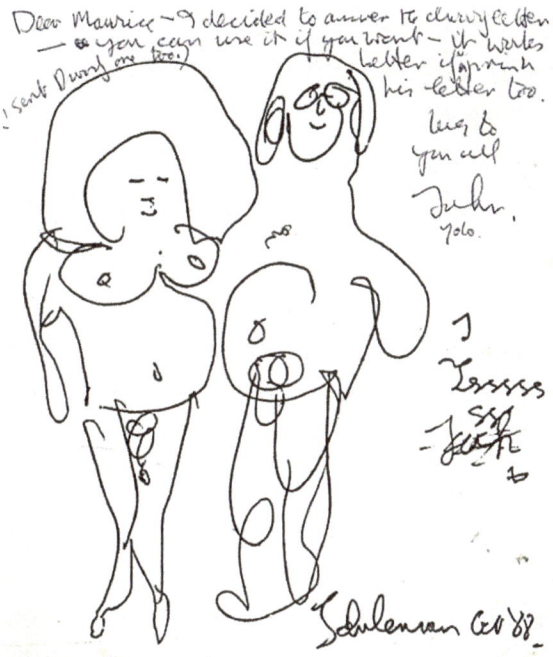

A handwritten and signed note to a journalist who had written a story about John. He has penned it on a copy of a drawing of both he and Yoko, from 1968.

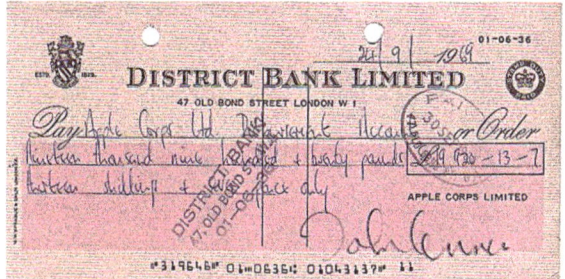

District Bank Limited check made out in another hand to Apple Corp Ltd. and signed by John Lennon. The date on the check is September 24, 1969.

National Westminster Bank Limited check filled out in another hand and signed by John, dated October 14, 1970.

JOHN LENNON

Original movie ticket for *A Hard Day's Night,* 1964, signed by John ten years later in 1974. He also added a face doodle and the date.

A dollar bill signed on the reverse by John Lennon in 1974.

John Lennon's *Walls and Bridges* album cover signed and dedicated by John in 1974 and added his own artwork.

A record award from 93KHJ radio for the song "Whatever Gets You Through The Night" that achieved #1 status in 1974.

JOHN LENNON

An 8x10 photo of a young John, signed by Lennon in 1974. I later had the photographer, Jurgen Vollmer, also sign the photo at the top when he was at Planet Hollywood in Indianapolis.

A nice signature of John on a Bloomingdales business card from New York in the mid 1970s.

Sgt Pepper stereo album cover signed by John Lennon in 1974, and later signed by Ringo Starr during one of his All Star Band tours in the mid to late 1990s.

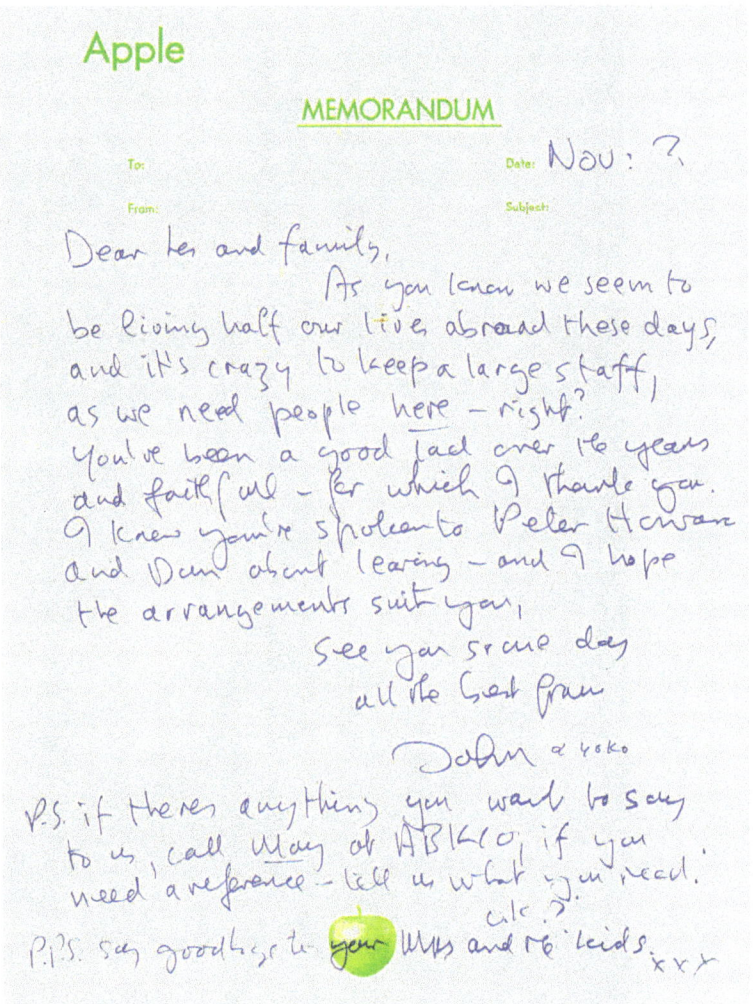

John's nice handwritten letter on Apple Memorandum stationery, November 1973.

JOHN LENNON

A rare stage play handbill for *Sgt. Pepper On the Road* (A Rock Spectacle), signed on the front by John Lennon in 1974, along with the original flyer.

JOHN LENNON

John Lennon's Grammy presentation medal incased in a wooden box. This was presented to John for appearing on the 1975 Grammy Awards. John donated this to an Indiana charity and I then purchased it from them. Plus, John Lennon's personally owned and worn black beret. John has also signed the beret. I lightened the image to see the signature. John can be seen wearing the beret at the 1975 Grammy Awards when he was a presenter.

THE HELPING HAND MARATHON

In May of 1975, John Lennon was invited by Larry Kane, an old friend from The Beatles days, to attend *The Helping Hand Marathon* in Philadelphia, Pa. While there, John even appeared on TV as a weatherman in his typical humor. He really gave his time and support to the event all weekend by signing autographs for a charitable contribution, including his latest album, *Rock and Roll,* as well as 45 picture sleeves of "Mind Games." As you can see, John was open to signnig anything fans set in front of him. The following are a sampling of the items I owned that were signed at that event.

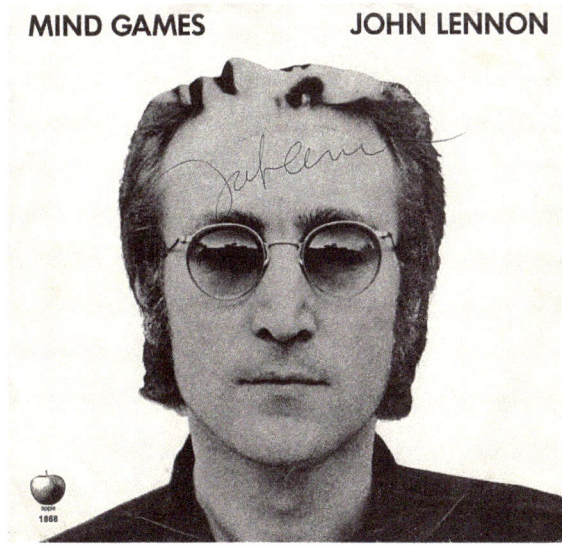

THE HELPING HAND MARATHON (CONTINUED)

BEATLES

THE HELPING HAND MARATHON (CONTINUED)

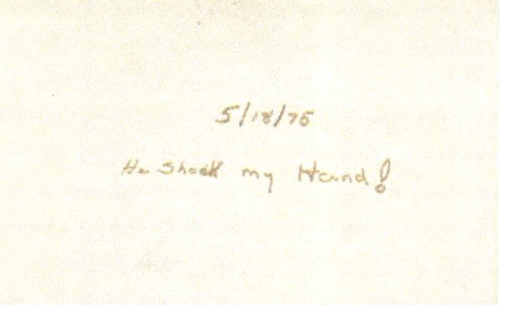

5/18/75
He Shook my Hand!

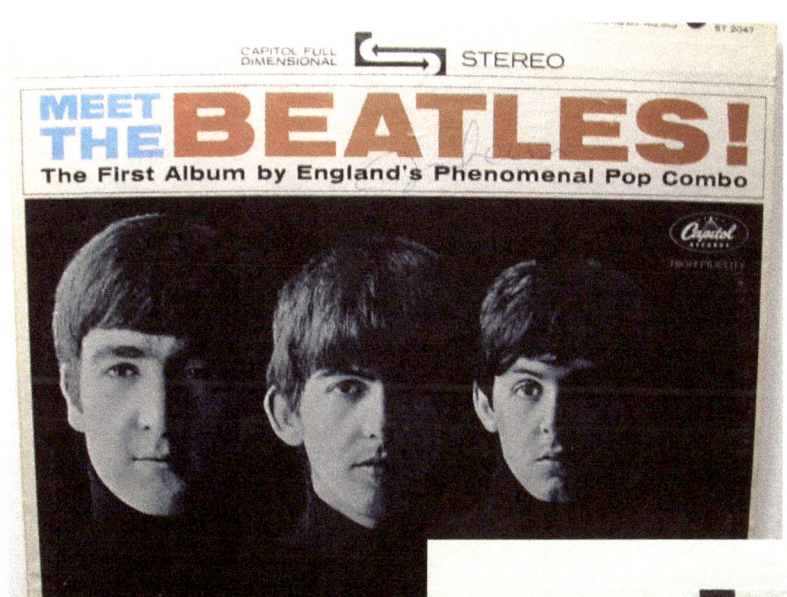

JOHN LENNON

John Lennon's personally owned and worn Home shirt with a picture of John wearing the shirt in the studio in 1975.

Full image art cell of John from The Beatles movie *Yellow Submarine* signed by John Lennon in the 1970s.

JOHN LENNON

A signed Playbill for the Merce Cunningham Dance performance in New York, which John and Yoko attended in 1977. A picture of John signing accompanies the playbill.

JOHN LENNON

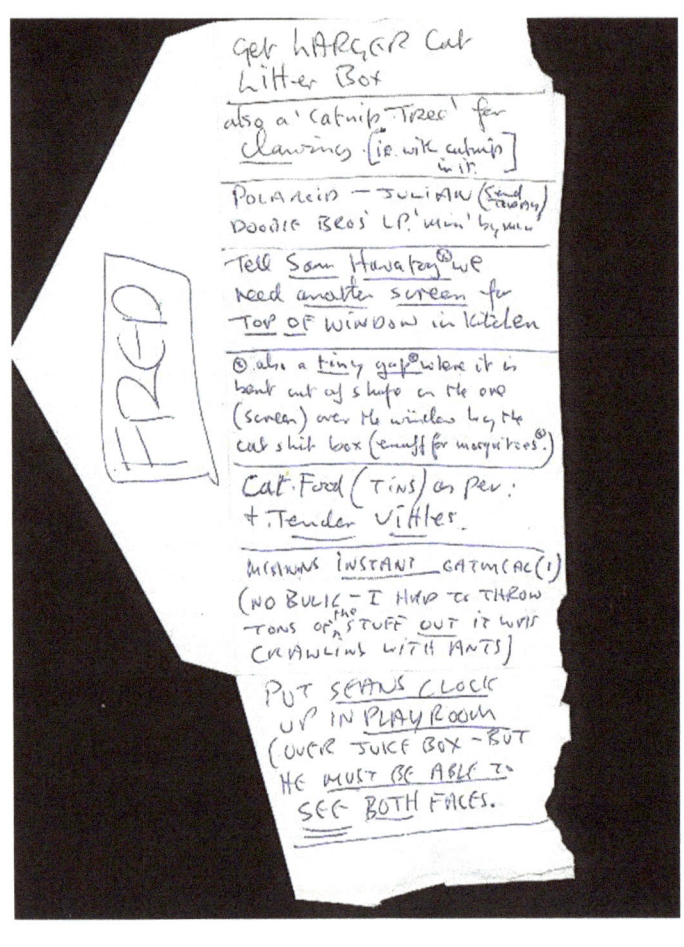
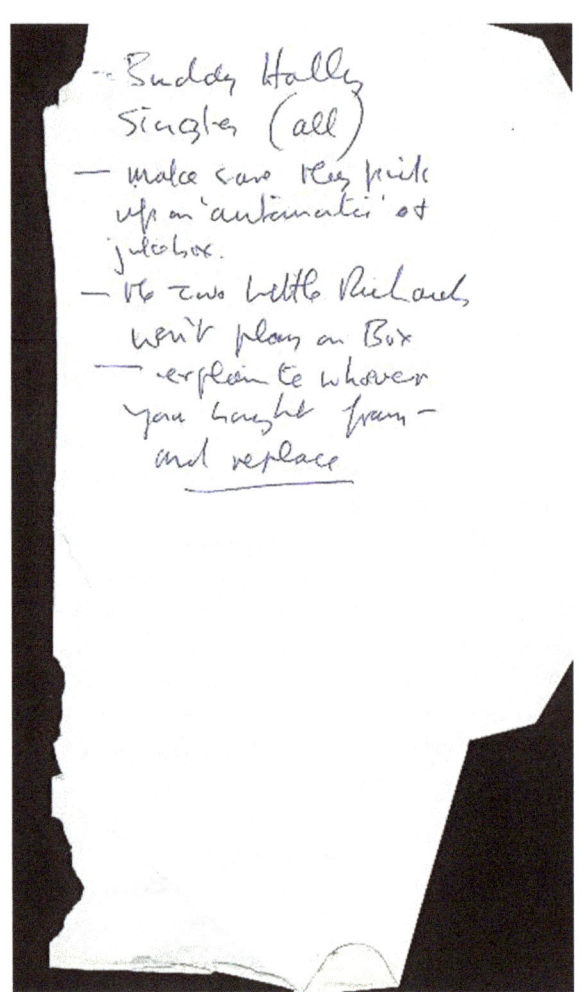

A handwritten "to do" list to John's assistant and friend, Fred Seaman, written on both sides of an envelope in 1980.

"Xmas Song" by Sean Ono Lennon '79

Handwritten postcard to Rosa Lopez and family in 1979, wishing them a "Merry Xmas" and "Happy 80s'". Rosa was John and Yoko's maid at the Dakota from 1973–1980.

JOHN LENNON

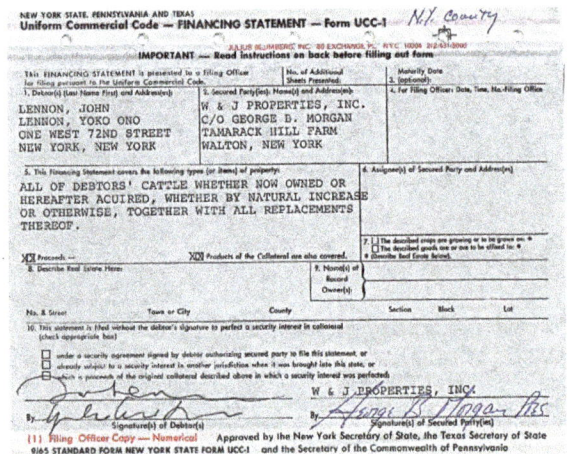
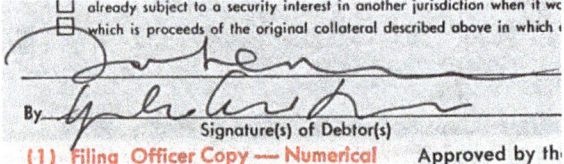

A finance statement from New York County Document, with Dakota address, signed by John Lennon and Yoko Ono in the late 1970s.

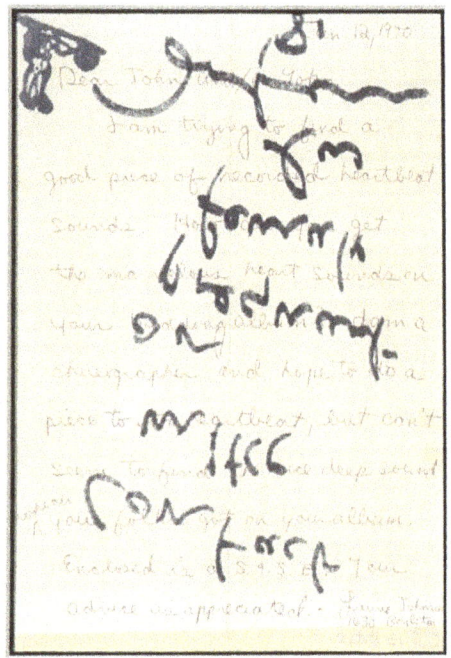
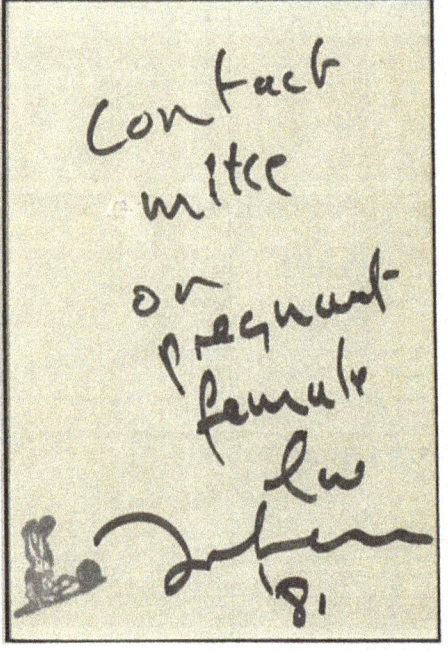

This is a "better late than never" item. A fan wrote to John in 1970, enquiring how to get the same heartbeat sounds he was achieving on his recordings at that time. Ten years later, John answered her letter, signed, dated it, and added a sketch.

While recording in the studio for what would be John's final recordings in 1980, he often went to the studio lounge to relax and do what came naturally — draw! An engineer at the studio saw John do his artwork and compared him to Picasso. He asked John if he could have some of his drawings and if he would also sign them, which he politely did.

JOHN LENNON

John and Yoko's final album before his passing, titled *Double Fantasy,* was released on November 17, 1980. To promote the album, John signed them for friends, executives, etc. including this one. Very few have surfaced.

A very lucky fan wrote John in late 1980 and he answered and signed this index card, adding the year and face doodle. It also includes the postdated December 1, 1980 envelope. I purchased this from the recipient and he told me he received it in the mail on December 10, two days after John was assassinated.

JOHN LENNON

John Lennon and Yoko Ono promotional 16x20 color prints matted and distributed by Polydor Records for the posthumous release of Milk and Honey, released in 1983.

JOHN LENNON'S LAST CONCERT APPEARANCE

On November 28th 1974, Thanksgiving Night during Elton John's encore, John Lennon came on stage at Madison Square Garden to do a few numbers with Elton and the band. This magical night also reunited John with Yoko. The following are items I collected from this event and once owned. They included the original newspaper concert review from the *New York Times*, the actual set list with the changes to support John's appearance, Elton John's stage outfit he wore that night (was on display for two years at The Rock and Roll Hall of Fame museum in Cleveland, Ohio), and a dollar bill signed by both John Lennon and Elton John obtained after the concert when the entire entourage went to a bar. This is where the bartender requested their autographs and received them. Who knew this incredible event was going to be John Lennon's last concert appearance.

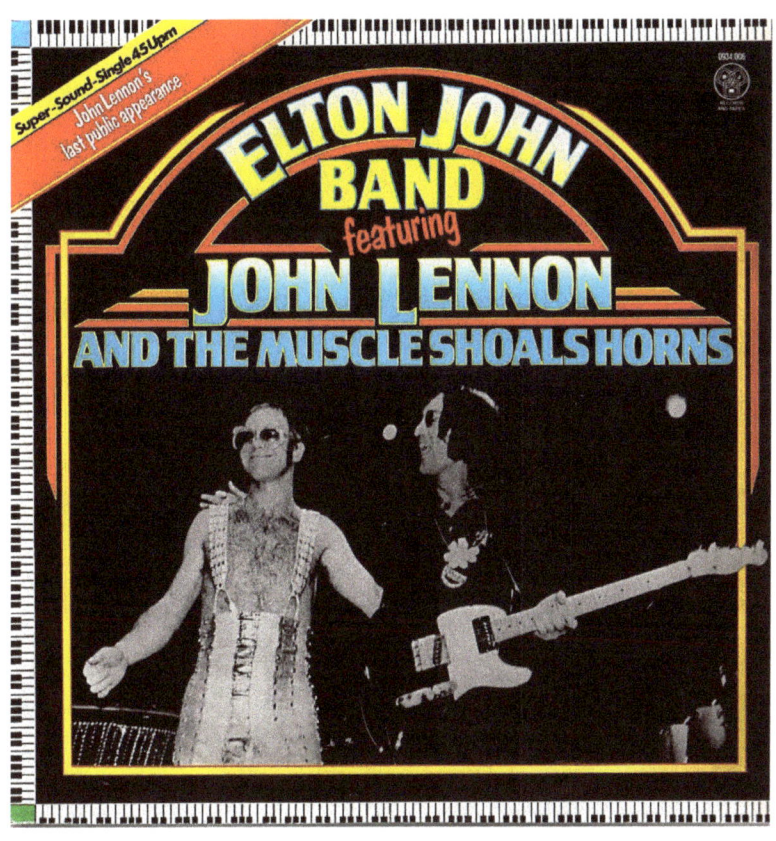

But when Mr. Lennon came on, the Garden was transformed. Not that the crowd hadn't given every indication of loving Mr. John and his music. But with Mr. Lennon, there was an electricity that sparked through the crowd long after Mr. Lennon had left the stage.

The two men sang three songs together: Mr. Lennon's current single, "Whatever Gets You Through the Night" as a simultaneously sung duet, the Beatles' "Lucy in the Sky With Diamonds" (Mr. John's current single), with Mr. John singing the verses and Mr. Lennon and the audience joining in for the choruses, and, in another duet, the early Beatles song "I Saw Her Standing There," which Mr. Lennon introduced as being by "an old fiancé of mine called Paul."

JOHN LENNON'S LAST CONCERT APPEARANCE (CONTINUED)

E.J. SET FOR U.S. TOUR 74.

1. FUNERAL
2. LOVE LIES
3. CANDLE IN THE WIND
4. GRIMSBY
5. ROCKET MAN
6. PILOT
7. BENNIE
8. DANIEL
9. GREY SEAL
10. GOODBYE YELLOW BRICK ROAD
11. BURN DOWN THE MISSION

12. YOUR SO STATIC
13. LUCY — *Whatever gets you thru'!* / *saw her standing there*
14. DON'T LET THE SUN — BRASS.
15. HONKY CAT
16. ALICE
17. SATURDAY NIGHT

18. CROCK ROCK
19. BITCH IS BACK. BRASS.
(20) (YOUR SONG)

---

www.rockstarsguitars.com
david brewis
pop memorabilia
37 Ravensdale Crescent, Gateshead, NE9 5YJ, England
phone 0191 4211831 mobile 07970 868572
e-mail david.brewis@lineone.net   6/8/01

Dear Tom,
I hope you enjoy owning the enclosed set list. It comes with a letter of provenance from Bill Harrison, who has owned it for many years. Originally working for George Harrison in the early 1970's, then as John Entwistle's bass technician in the later 1970's, Bill moved into hire and is now a tape archivist, amongst other things he does for major bands, such as tour logistics and storage. As an example, at Harrison's, Bill keeps all of Ringo's Ludwig drums from the Beatles years, in a controlled and secure environment. He is, lets say, the best at what he does.
Harrison's looks after all of the existing master tapes of the entire Rolling Stones output, and he also holds all of Elton John's work. This includes all live tapes, whether recorded for release or merely for reference. A box of approx. ten 1/4" stereo tapes of Elton John's 1974 US tour had been delivered from Elton's record label for safe keeping a long while back, although they were "old" then, and unlikely to be used. I believe that they still haven't been listened to! Bill says that the usual situation in these "field" recordings would be to throw in a set list rather than write a song listing on the box, as it was quicker, and reliable. Duly, at the bottom of the box, was this, the only known surviving set list from the tour, which had the additional songs performed with John Lennon at MSG added, John's last public concert. The reason that the paper is creased is that it sat under the tapes for so long!
This is truly a rare and historic item, and is the original article.

Good Luck!

David Brewis

JOHN LENNON'S LAST CONCERT APPEARANCE (CONTINUED)

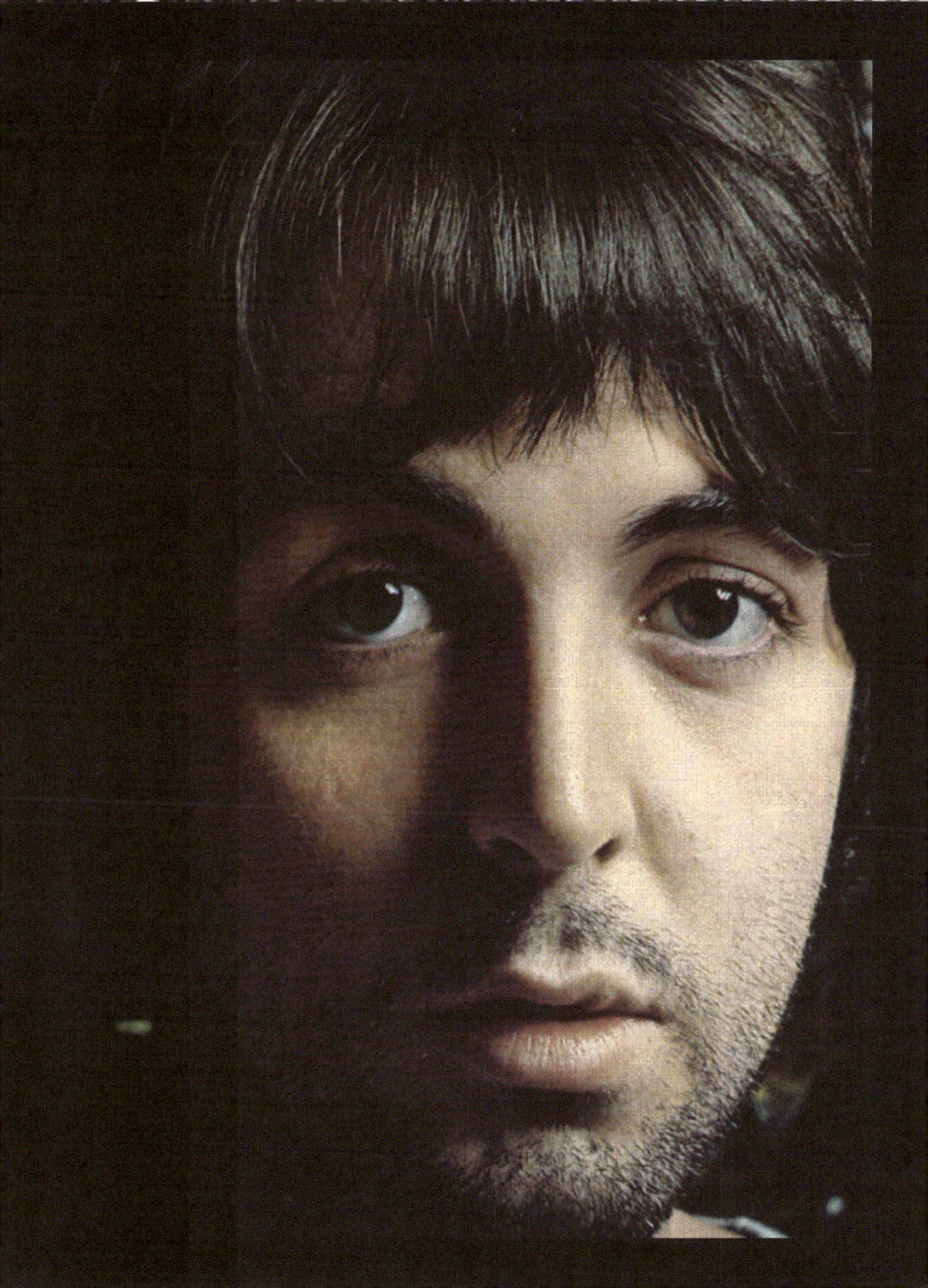

PAUL McCARTNEY

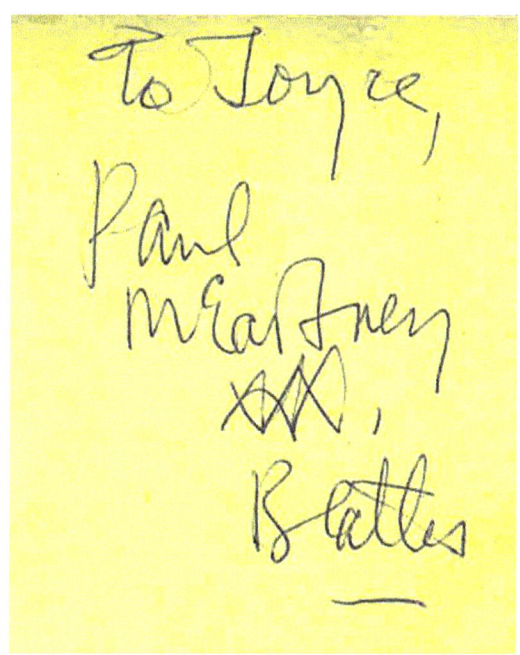

An early signature in an autograph book from Paul to a fan in late 1961.

Dear Elizabeth, (record we have made another) but it has not yet been released; it will be released in January. So I hope you're going to buy it!

Thanks,
love from
Paul McCartney
XXX.

This handwritten note was signed by Paul to a fan on the back of a Beatles Parlophone card in 1962.

▸ 81

PAUL McCARTNEY

A 1965 US Tour book page picturing Paul and a nice dedication with signature.

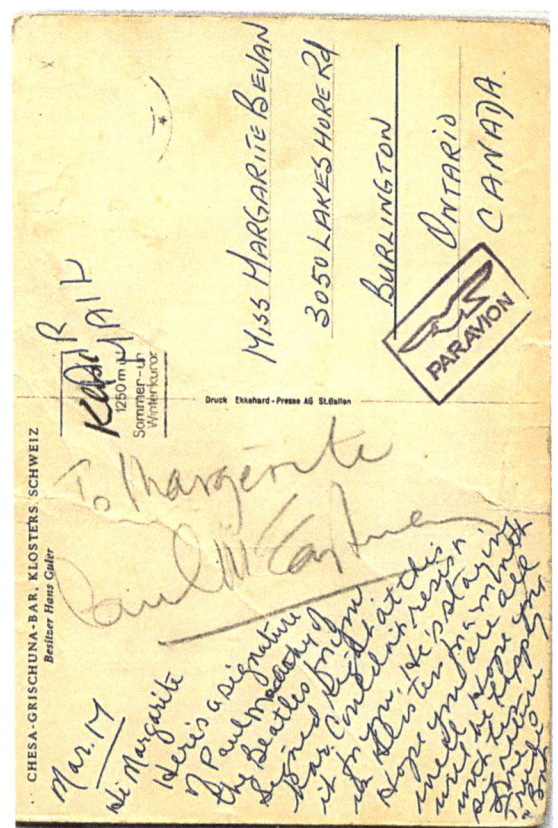

A postcard addressed to Canada from Switzerland, signed on the reverse with dedication by Paul McCartney. Autograph was obtained while Paul and then-girlfriend Jane Asher were on holiday in March 1966.

PAUL McCARTNEY

Paul McCartney signature matted from 1966.

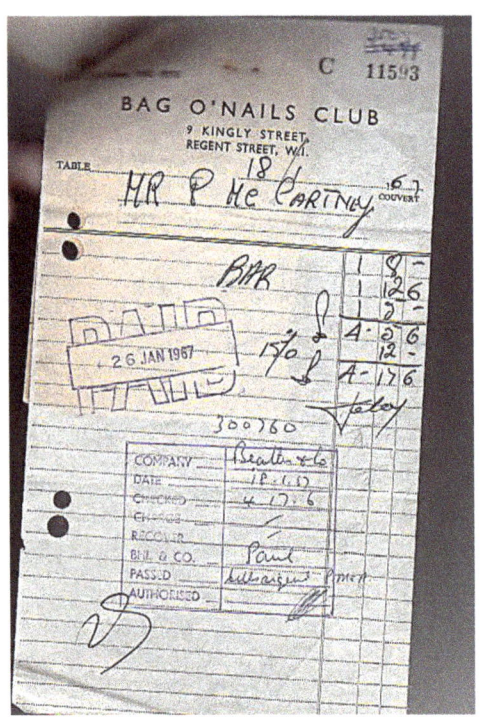

An extremely rare set of receipts from the Bag O' Nails music nightclub in London, with signatures of Paul on the receipts. This is the club where Paul met his first wife, Linda. These receipts are from 1967.

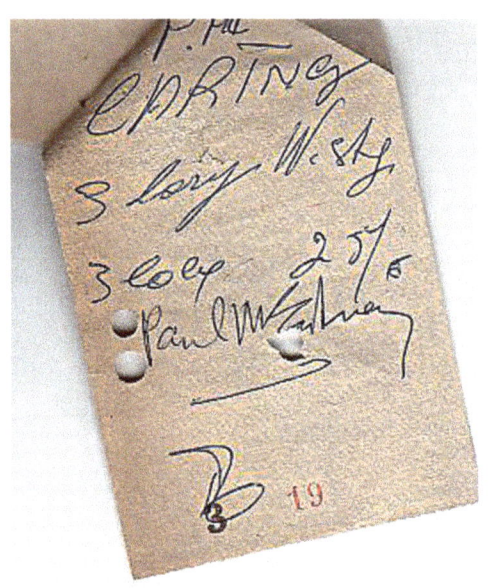

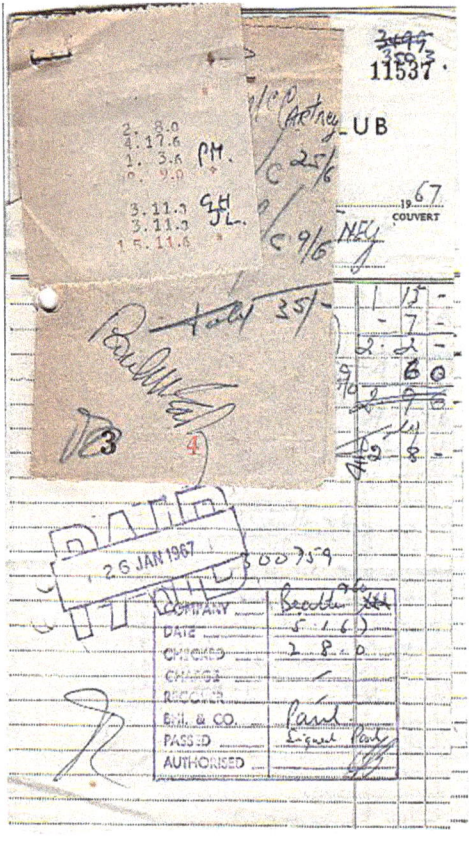

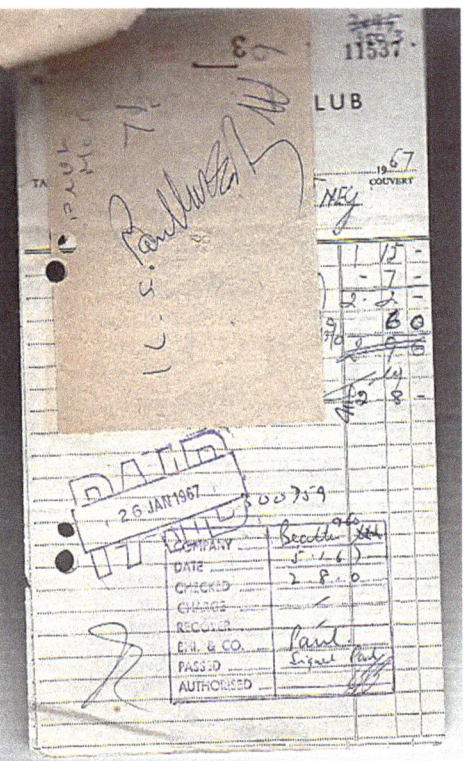

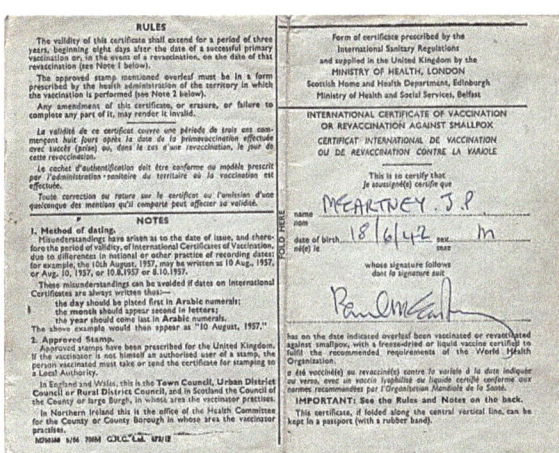

This is Paul's International Vaccination form from 1968. It was required for his and John Lennon's trip to New York to announce Apple Records in May of 1968.

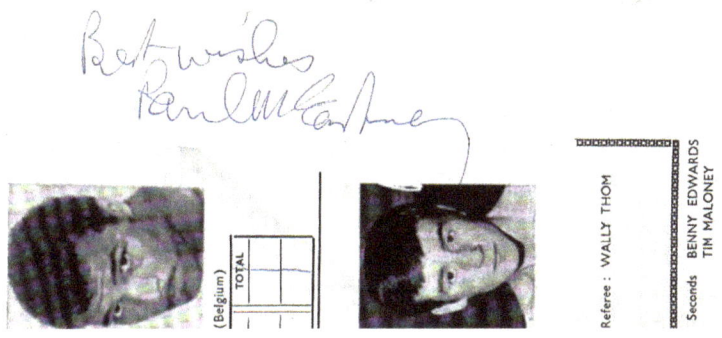

Boxing program signed on the inside page next to fighter John Conteh. Paul attended the boxing match in 1973. McCartney later met with the fighter and asked him if he would be on the cover of Band On The Run with other personalities, and Conteh agreed.

Paul McCartney and Wings color 8x10 signed by Paul, Linda, Denny Laine, Jimmy McCulloch, and Joe English in 1976.

A poster from the Venus and Mars album signed by Paul, Linda, Denny Laine and Jimmy McCulloch.

PAUL McCARTNEY

Linda's Pix for Seventy Six picture book and calendar, signed on an inside page by Paul McCartney and Linda McCartney.

PAUL McCARTNEY

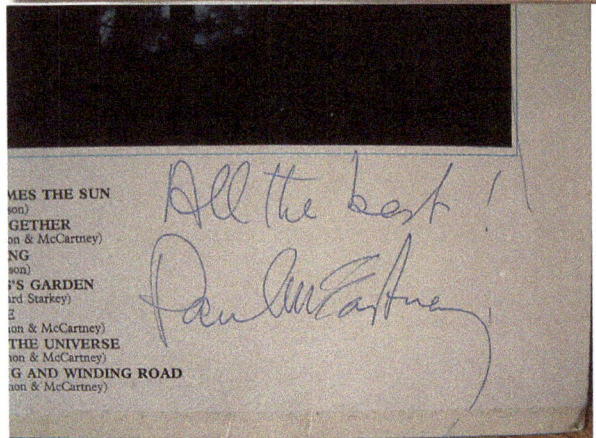

Beatles album cover *1967-1970* signed on the centerfold, inside bottom right by Paul McCartney.

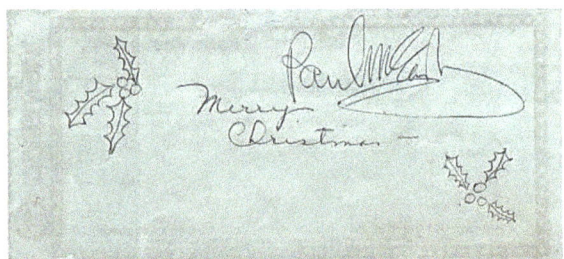

A money envelope for a Christmas gift to the recipient, who was also lucky enough to meet Paul McCartney and have him sign it.

PAUL McCARTNEY

Beatles album cover *1967-1970* signed on the front by Paul McCartney from the 1980s.

Thank You Very Much Mike McCartney's Family Album book signed and inscribed by Paul adding a smiley face and his brother who signed it Mike Mac on the testimonial page.

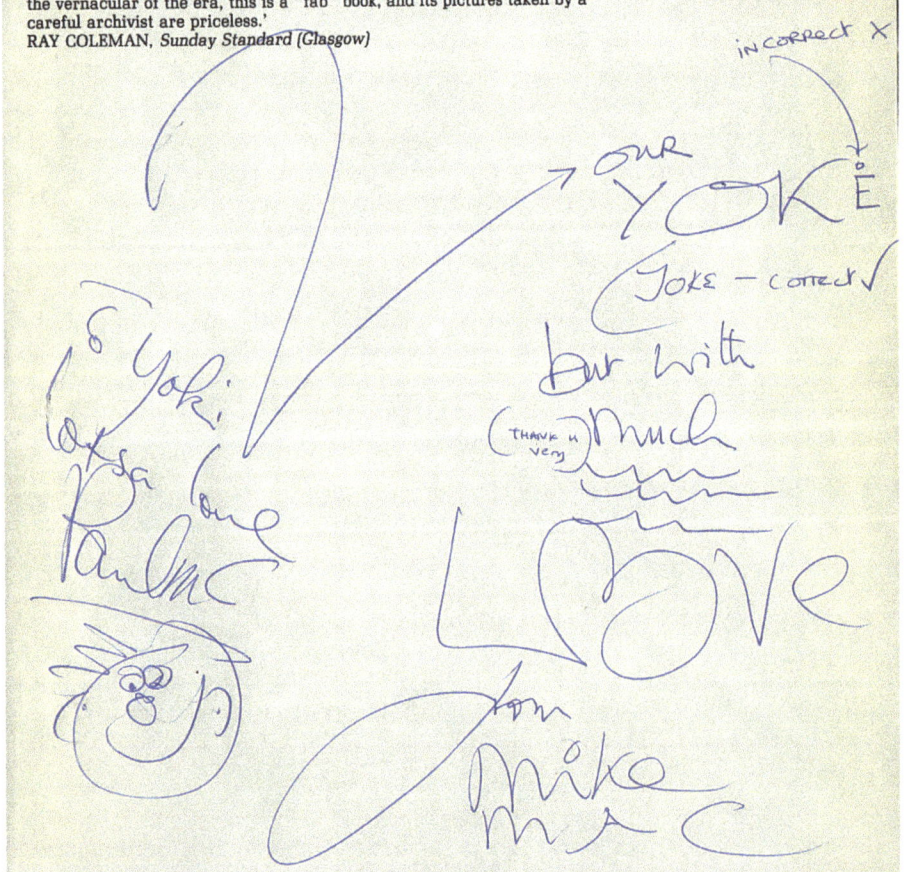

PAUL McCARTNEY

A copyright notice rider for 1976 McCartney Music, signed by Paul and Linda. On the reverse is information about Paul's song "Let Em In."

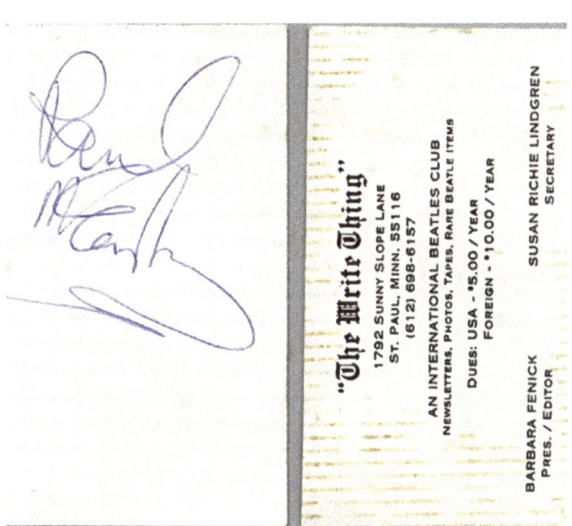

Barb Fenick president/editor of The Write Thing (International Beatles Club) was lucky enough to meet Paul and have him sign her business card on the reverse.

A nice signature of Paul McCartney on an autograph book page from 2/20/1980.

A 1982 re-release movie poster for *A Hard Day's Night* signed nicely by Paul McCartney in the early '80s.

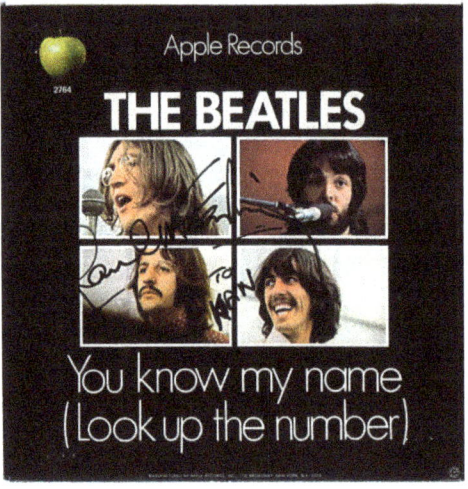

The Beatles picture sleeve for "Let It Be"/"You Know My Name," signed with inscription by Paul McCartney in the 1980s.

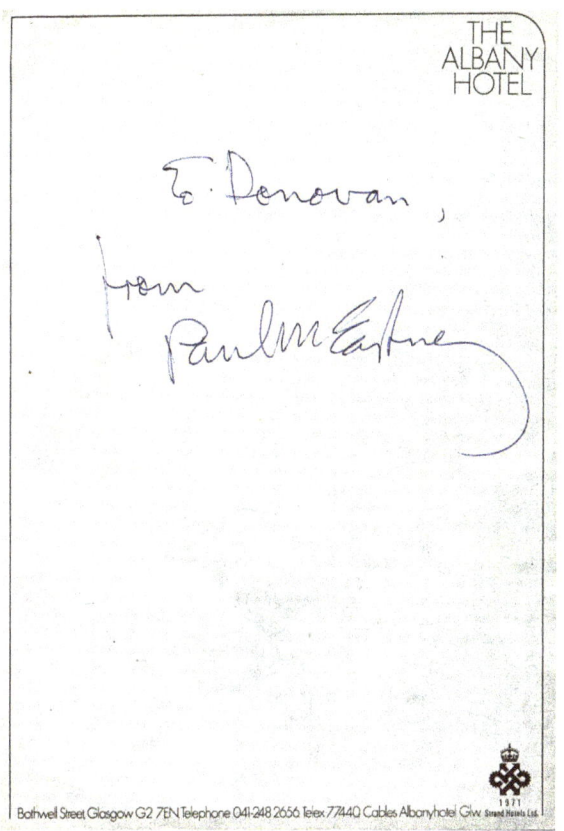

A pair of menus from different restaurants and years signed and dedicated by Paul McCartney.

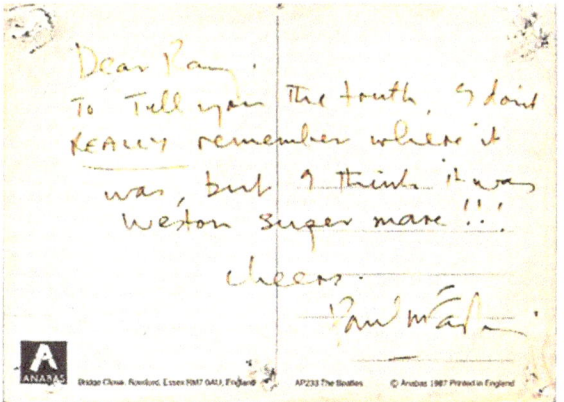

An original 1960s Beatles postcard with a handwritten note recalling the location where the photo was taken, signed by Paul after The Beatles Years.

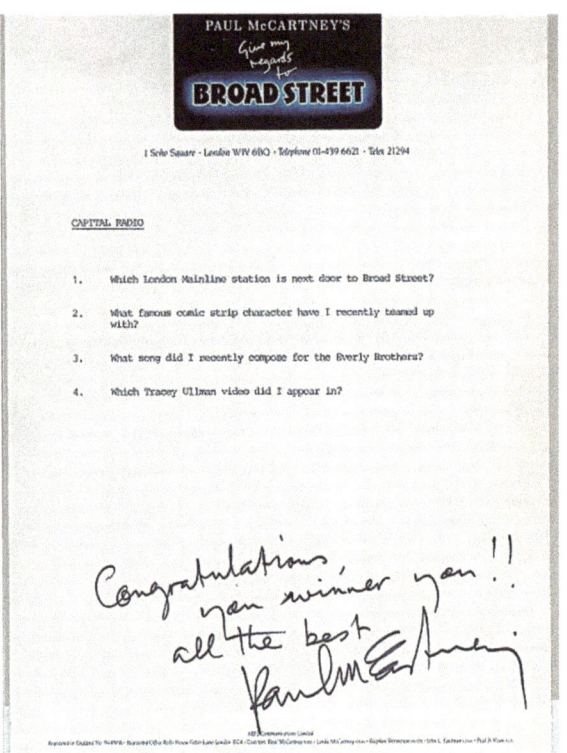

In 1984, to promote Paul's movie, *Give My Regards to Broadstreet,* a contest questionnaire was prepared and Paul has signed it and dedicated it to the winner of the contest.

A unique color photo of Paul McCartney made up like a clown that has been nicely signed by Paul with an inscription and added smiley face.

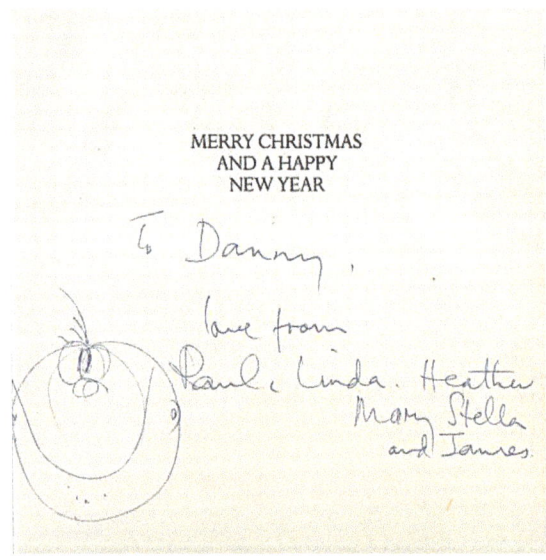

A Holiday greeting card to a family friend with all writing in the hand of Paul McCartney, who added a face doodle.

A Holiday greeting card signed by Paul McCartney, who also signed for Linda.

PAUL McCARTNEY

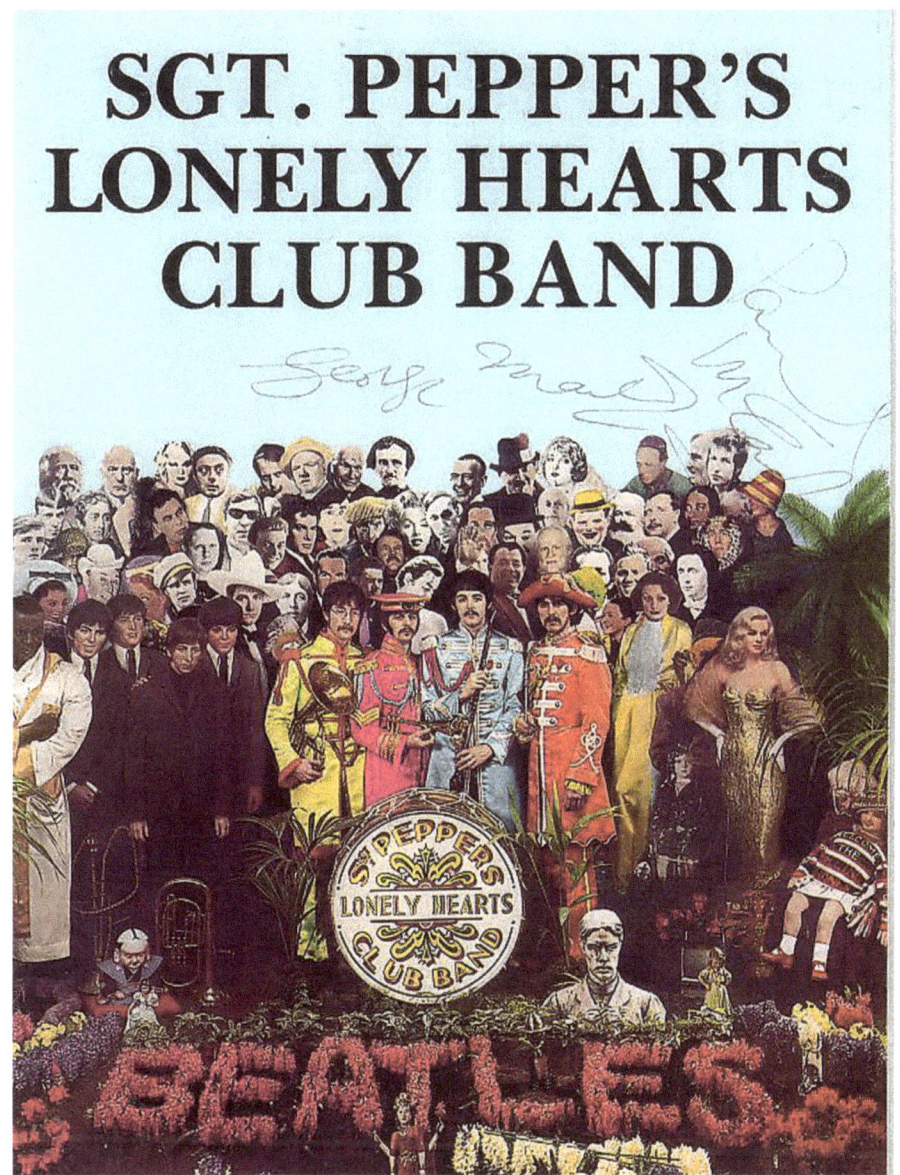

To Promote the 20th Anniversary of the release of *Sgt Pepper* in 1987, a press kit was also created and it is signed nicely by Paul McCartney and The Beatles longtime record producer George Martin.

A Hand drawn pencil sketch of flowers in a vase that has been dedicated and signed by Paul and Linda McCartney with the date at the top from 1990.

PAUL McCARTNEY

Paul McCartney's Fan club magazine, *Club Sandwich*, signed on the front by Paul, Linda, Mitch Mitchell (Jimi Hendrix Experience) and Beatles movies co-star Victor Spinetti in 1991

McCartney's album *Unplugged*, released in 1991, signed and dedicated by Paul on the front cover.

A nice Stratocaster Squire guitar signed by Paul McCartney on the pic- guard circa early '90s.

PAUL McCARTNEY

Very seldom do you get the opportunity to own something from a friend or family member of an artist, so I was fortunate enough to obtain this incredible pic guard signed by Paul along with the envelope the guard was housed in. Paul dedicated the envelope and added a smiley face. Later it was applied on a Hoefner Bass. A few years later, I was again lucky enough to obtain another pic guard signed by Paul for a family member and also applied to a Hoefner It was great to have the opportunity to own both of these historical items in my collection.

PAUL MCCARTNEY'S *FLOWERS IN THE DIRT* WORLD TOUR 1989–1990

A promotional postcard signed nicely by Paul McCartney from 1989 around the release of *Flowers In The Dirt* album.

Paul McCartney 1989–1990 US tour book, signed by Paul, with pictures the day of the signing.

The inner yellow sleeve from the album *Flowers in the Dirt* signed by Paul McCartney, Linda McCartney, Wix Wickens, Hamish Stuart, Robbie McIntosh, and Chris Whitten.

PAUL MCCARTNEY'S *FLOWERS IN THE DIRT* WORLD TOUR 1989–1990
(CONTINUED)

Paul McCartney free handout booklet for 1989–1990 concert tour signed on the front cover by Paul and obtained during the tour. What makes this special it that I purchased this from one of Paul's mates from the Liverpool days.

Paul McCartney free handout booklet for 1989–1990 concert tour, signed nicely on the front cover by Paul. Obtained during the tour.

PAUL McCARTNEY'S *FLOWERS IN THE DIRT* WORLD TOUR 1989–1990
(CONTINUED)

A promotional poster advertising Paul McCartney America 1989, signed by Paul from 1989.

PAUL McCARTNEY'S *FLOWERS IN THE DIRT* WORLD TOUR 1989–1990
(CONTINUED)

Poster from *Flowers In The Dirt World Tour Pack* from 1989, signed by Paul McCartney, Linda McCartney, Wix Wickens, Hamish Stuart, Robbie McIntosh, and Chris Whitten.

PAUL McCARTNEY

A Program from Paul McCartney's *Liverpool Oratorio* in 1991. This is the program from that event autographed by McCartney next to his image.

PAUL McCARTNEY

The New World Tour handout program signed by Paul on the front cover from 1993. This was given to fans who purchased the LIPA package that included the sound check and the concert in 1993.

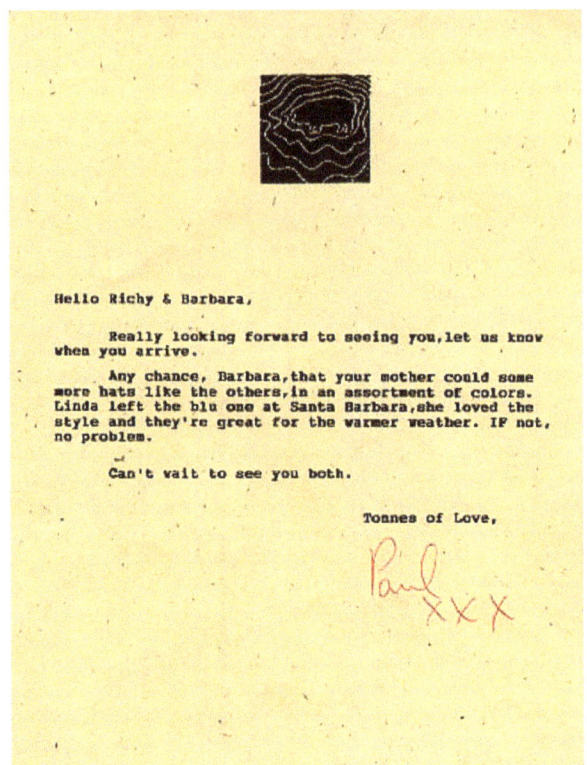

Above, two exceptionally rare letters from Paul to fellow Beatle Ringo Starr in the 1990s.

Paul McCartney's *Run Devil Run* CD cover signed on the front in 1999.

After the passing of Linda McCartney in 1997, a project she was working on with Paul, *Wide Prairie,* was released in 1998. On the inside CD cover, Paul has signed on his image and placed a heart over Linda. Very few signed copies of this ever surfaced.

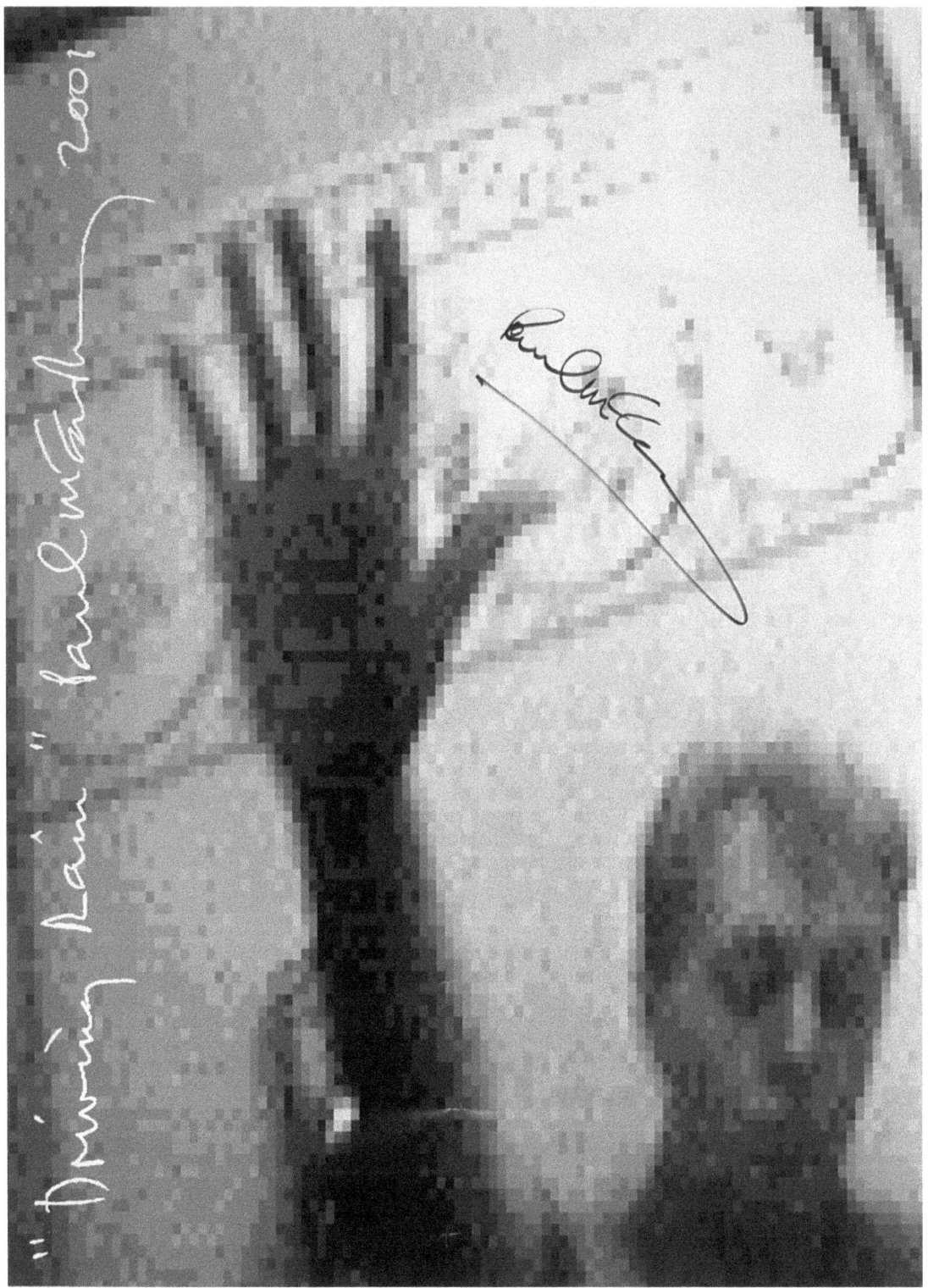

Promotional posters for the album *Driving Rain* released in 2001 signed by Paul.

PAUL MEETS HIS FANS
AT BOOK SIGNINGS FOR PAINTINGS (2000) AND BLACKBIRD SINGING (2001)

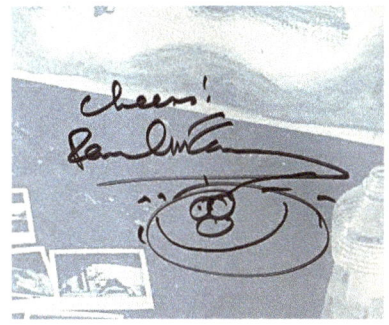

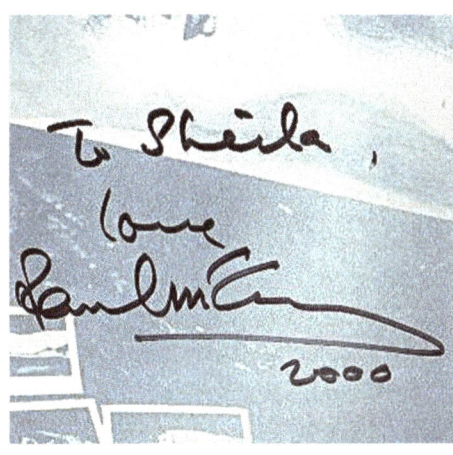

PAUL MEETS HIS FANS

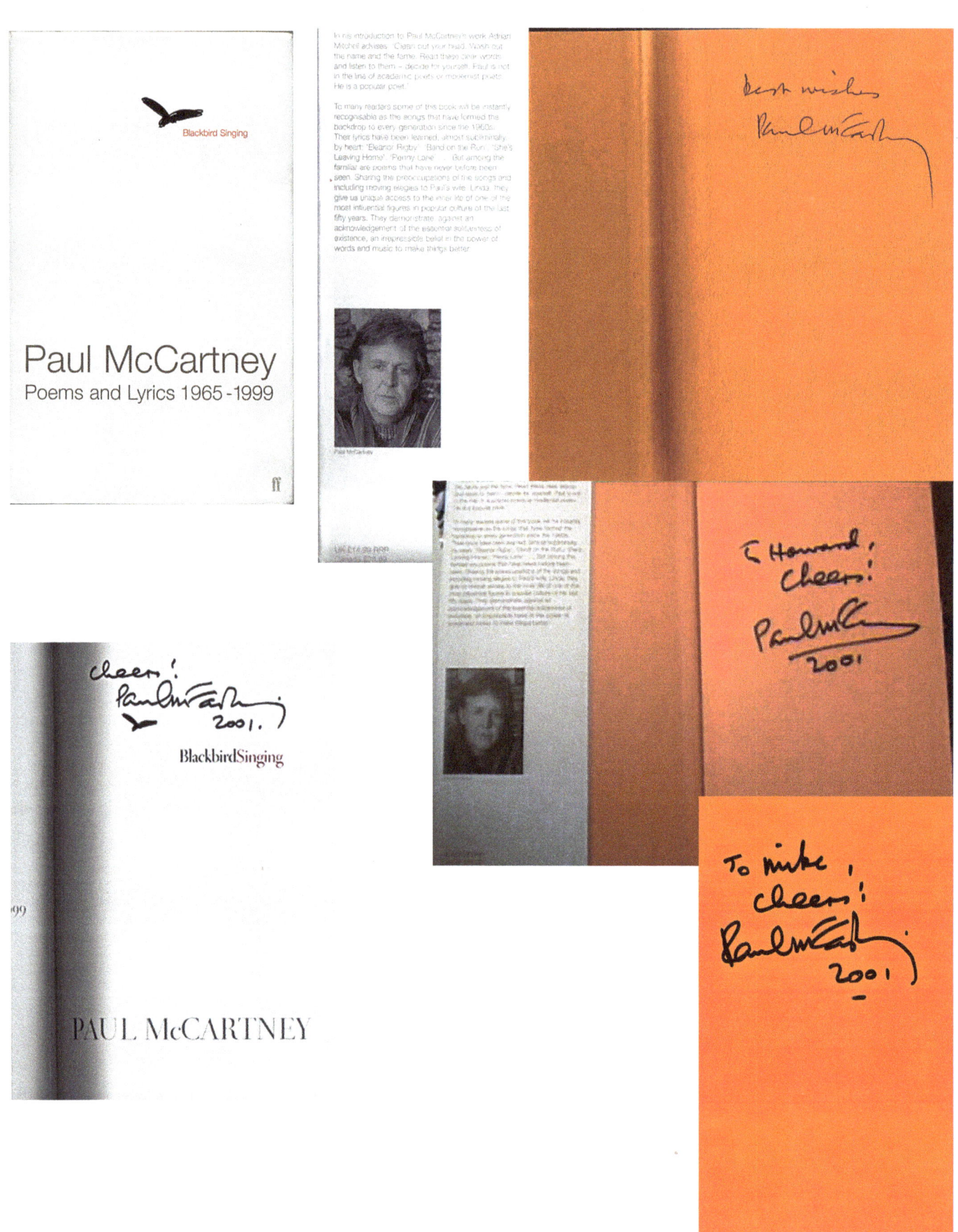

PAUL SIGNS FOR HIS FANS
IN LIVERPOOL AND THE WORLD THRU THE YEARS

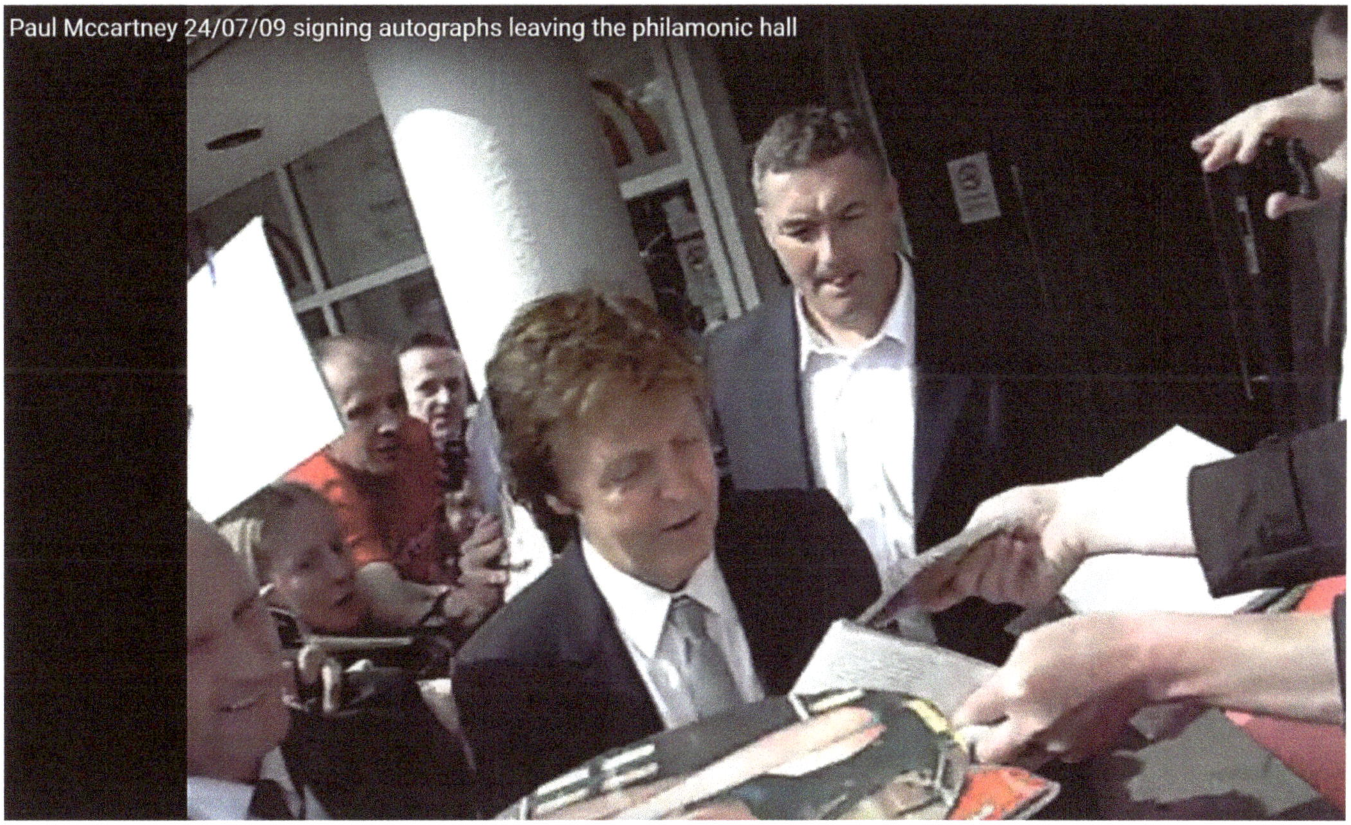

Paul Mccartney 24/07/09 signing autographs leaving the philamonic hall

PAUL SIGNS FOR HIS FANS

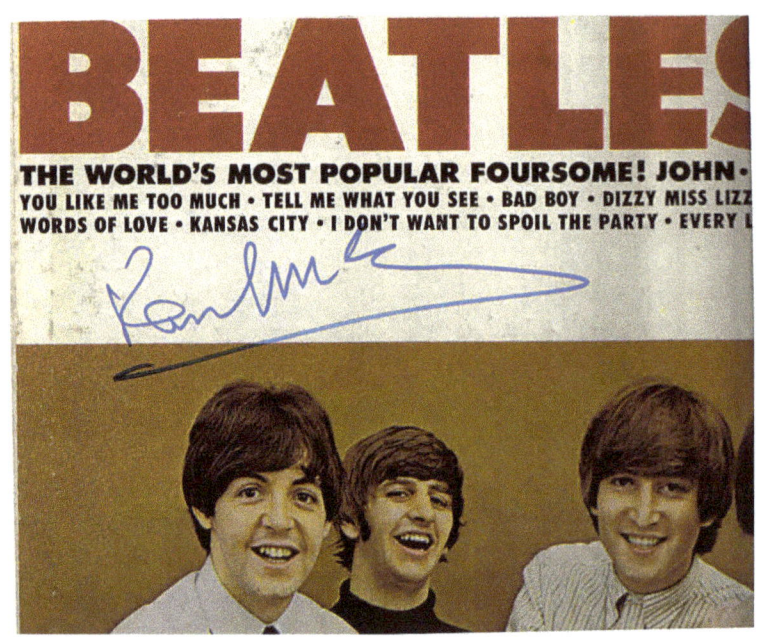

PAUL SIGNS FOR HIS FANS

PAUL SIGNS FOR HIS FANS

PAUL SIGNS FOR HIS FANS

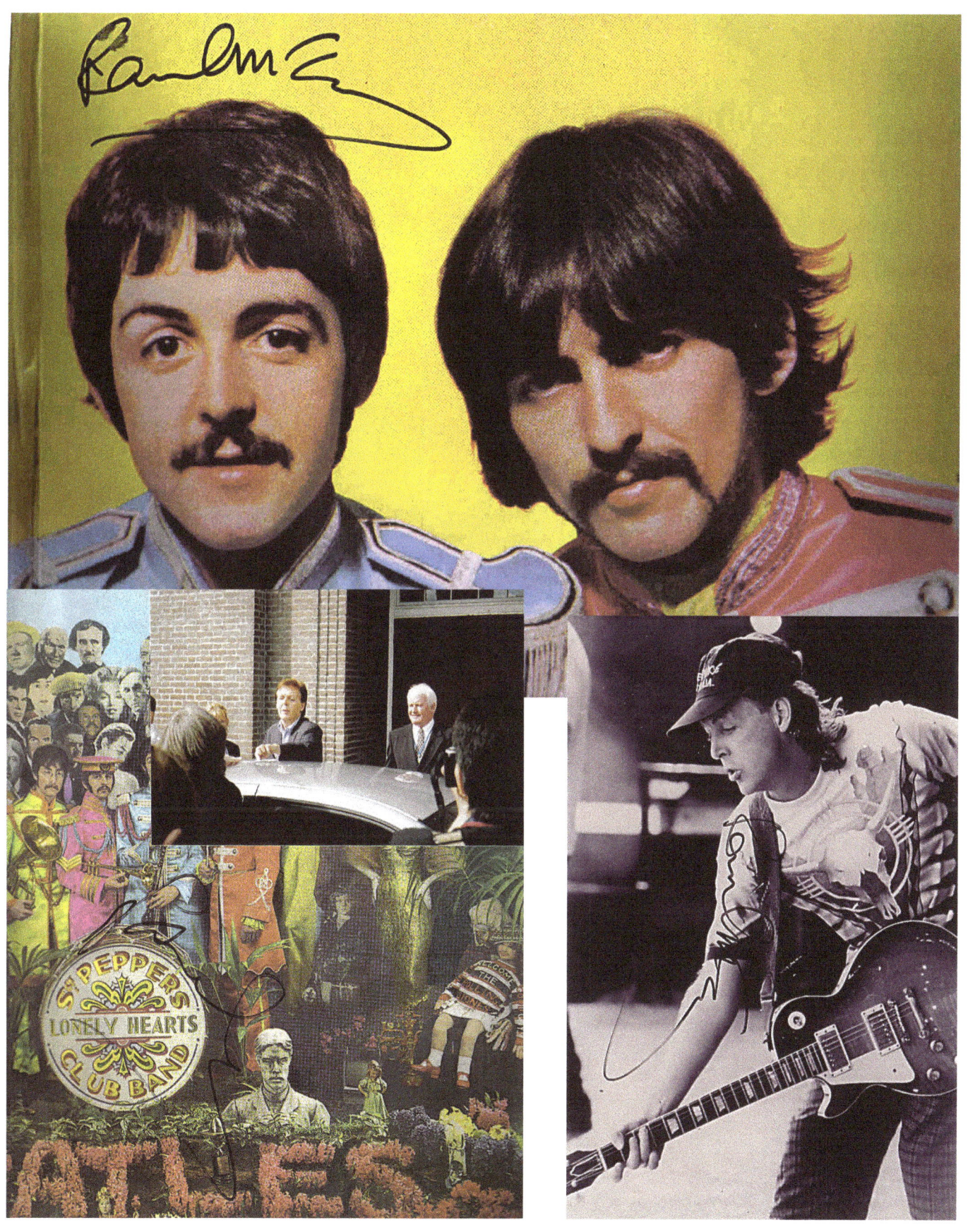

PAUL SIGNS FOR HIS FANS

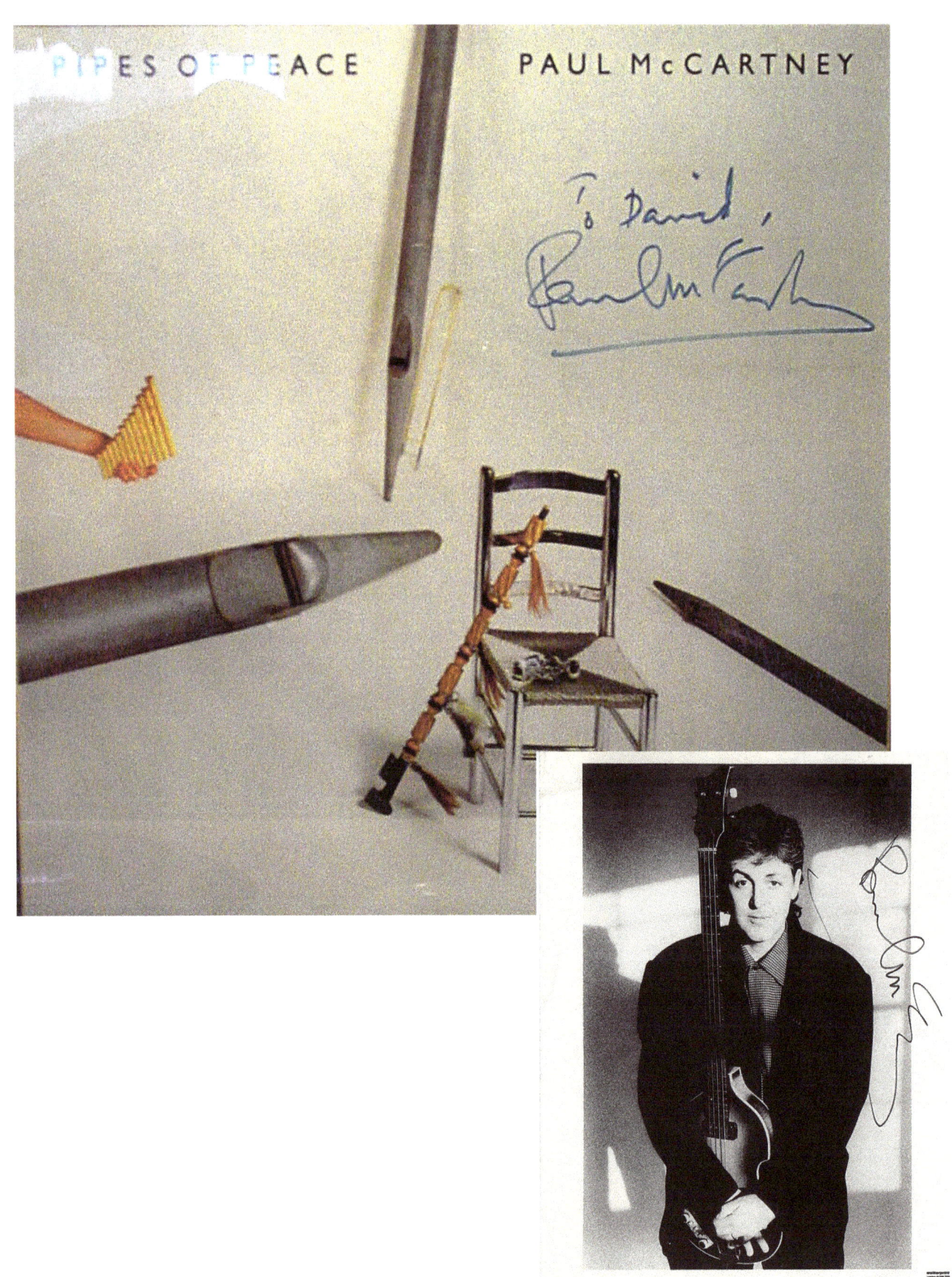

PAUL SIGNS FOR HIS FANS

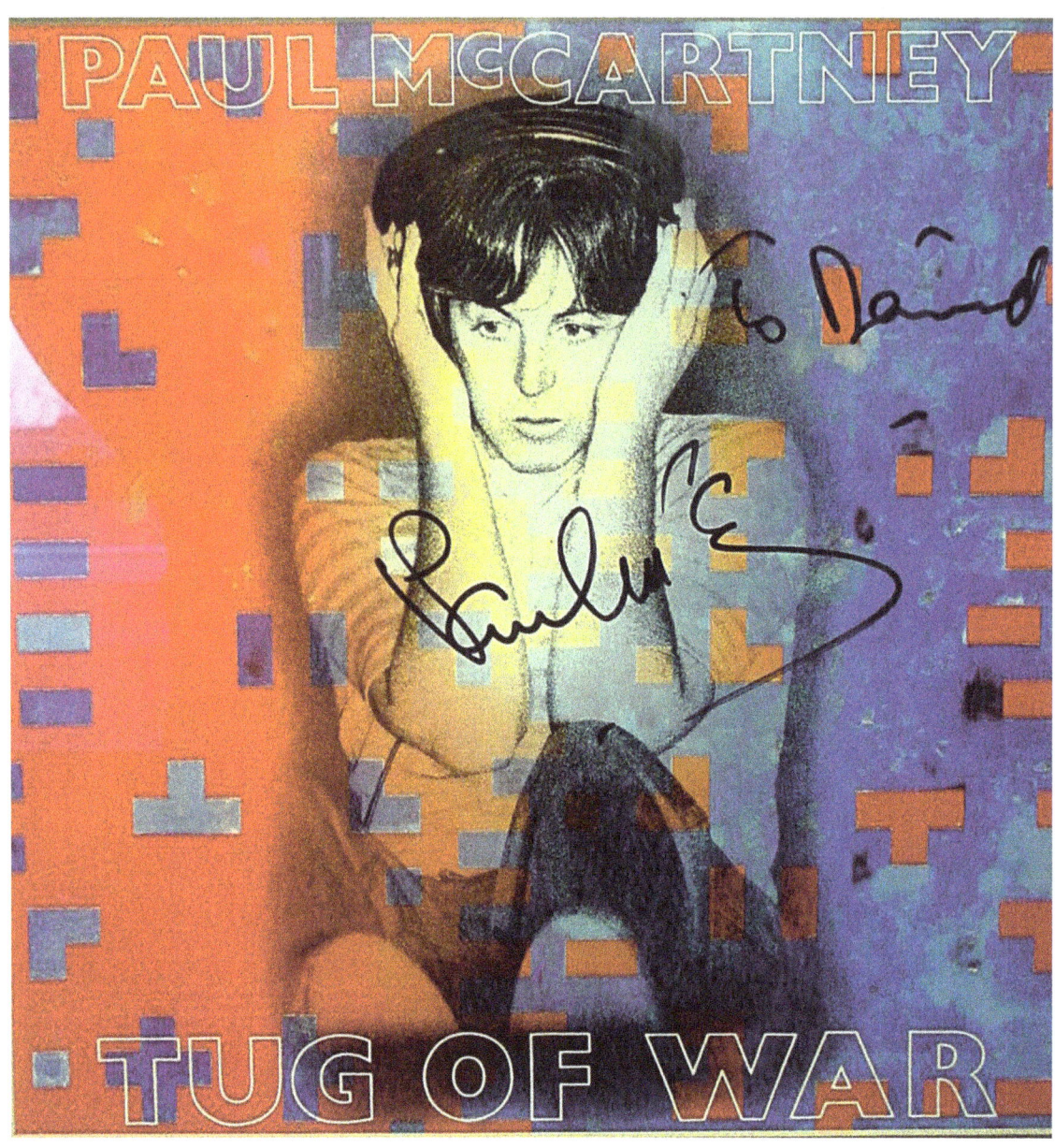

PAUL SIGNS FOR HIS FANS

My Memories of

Beatlefest

My Memories of *Beatlefest*

In 1982 I attended my first Beatles Fest Convention. Remember those were the days before the internet and ebay and the only way you could celebrate The Beatles with friends old and new was attending these conventions once a year. For me it was Chicago. There was something simple to it all looking forward to every year and knowing there was a convention just about your favorite group and everyone having a good time in the celebration.

My wife Mary and I attended all the Chicago fests from 1982–2010. The nice part of the these occasions were the friendships we developed with fellow fans, seeing the special guests and experiencing the massive Flea Market of Beatles memorabilia on display and for sale. I always looked forward to the Beatles auction on Saturday and Sunday because you never knew what collectible gems would be in there to bid on.

On other occasions we were also fortunate enough to attend the fests in Los Angeles in 1989 when Paul McCartney was in town to play Los Angeles's fabulous Forum which created an extra buzz the entire weekend. We also attended the fest in New Jersey where we met people for the first time I had only spoken to previously

on the phone. The real highlight for us was meeting the Beatles movie producer Walter Shenson and inviting us to be in a documentary about the movie *A Hard Day's Night*. It was released and hosted by Phil Collins and yes we are in the documentary. Walter has now passed but was a true gentleman and we enjoyed our conversation with him immensely.

In 2005, with the notoriety of my collection over the years, I was honored to be associated with The Beatle Brunch team featuring Joe Johnson who does the weekly broadcast celebrating the music and lives of the Fab Four.

MY MEMOMRIES OF BEATLEFEST

He would often feature me in broadcast and post stories about my collection on their website. To promote the Beatle Brunch, Joe and BB family would attend the fest and was kind enough to invite me to the party to set up items from my Beatles collection.

Those were special times for me to interact with fans and collectors who enjoyed The Beatles and viewing my collection over the years.

The years have passed and it has been years since I attended but I will never forget the fond memories these conventions provided and the group that inspired them.

Tom Fontaine

MY MEMOMRIES OF BEATLEFEST

Top row, left, Mary with Paul's guitarist and former Pretender, Robbie McIntosh in 2000; right, Original Apple Scruff Girl, Lizzie Bravo, in 2003.

Second row, left, Beatles Shea Stadium Promoter Sid Bernstein in 2001; right, At the flea market with Tracks UK owner Paul Wane in 2001.

Third row, right, Paul's bass player and former member of The Average White band , Hamish Stuart in 2000; right, At the flea Market in 2001.

Fourth row, Photographer and friend to The Beatles in the early days in Germany, Klauss Voormann in 2001.

MY MEMOMRIES OF BEATLEFEST

Top, downstairs at the Flea market in 2002. Bottom, left, Mary with Mark Hudson from the Hudson brothers in 2003; right, Mary with singer Donavon in 2003.

MY MEMOMRIES OF BEATLEFEST

Above, Mary with John Lennon's original group The Quarrymen in 2007. Bottom right, Mary with Wings Guitarist Denny Laine in 2005.

125

MY MEMOMRIES OF BEATLEFEST

Set up at The Beatle Brunch table in 2006.

Beatle Brunch table in August 2008.

MY MEMOMRIES OF BEATLEFEST

Victor Spinetti in 2007. He appeared in all three movies with The Beatles.

Below, Mary with George Harrison's former wife Patti Boyd in 2008.

▶ 127

MY MEMOMRIES OF BEATLEFEST

Above, Beatle Brunch table in 2009.

Right, Mary with former Ronnette, Ronnie Spector in 2009.

MY MEMOMRIES OF BEATLEFEST

Beatle Brunch table 2010.

Below, left, Mary with Beatle Bruch radio host Joe Johnson in 2008.

GEORGE HARRISON

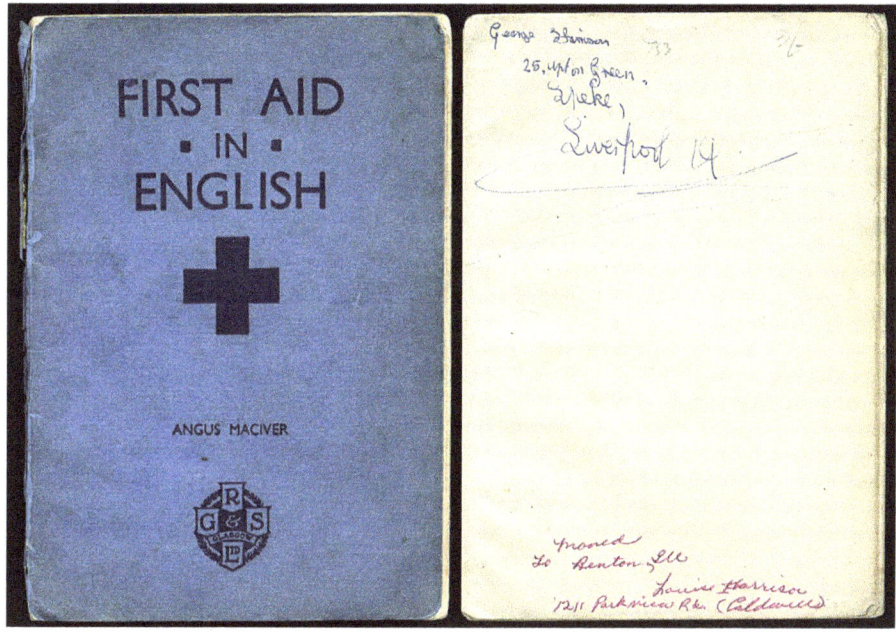

George Harrison's personally owned first aid book, used at the Liverpool grammar school George attended.

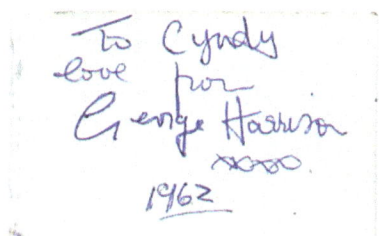

George's signature on a small autograph book page from 1962.

A Beatles Promotional Card with a nice handwritten note by George Harrison to a fan on the reverse. He also mentions their latest release "She Loves You" in 1963.

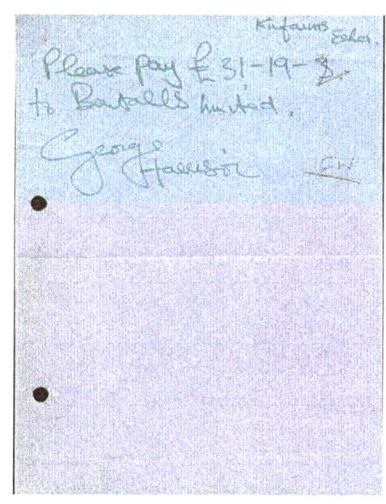

A handwritten note on color stationery, signed in 1966.

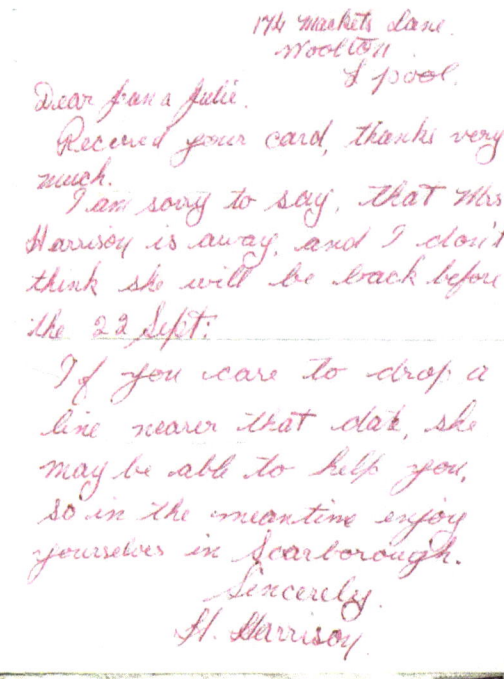

Often George's parents would get fan mail and would be gracious enough to respond. Here are two letters from George's mother and father, postmarked 1964.

The Beatles 1964 US Tour book dedicated and signed by George Harrison.

A Polaroid photo of a girl on the beach and also was the recipient of George Harrison's autograph in 1967 next to her image.

GEORGE HARRISON

A Beatles monthly book from 1966, signed in the centerfold on his image by George.

GEORGE HARRISON

To John, Mary and Hayley — (I hope you are all well)
Christmas Greetings
from
George and Patti

P.S. I don't know if you have my new phone number, but it is ESHER 64259. ta...

A very nice Christmas card from George and Patti Harrison to actress Haley Mills and family, including actor John Mills. Quite rare.

THE SOLO YEARS
CHECKS, DOCUMENTS, LETTERS, AND RECEIPTS

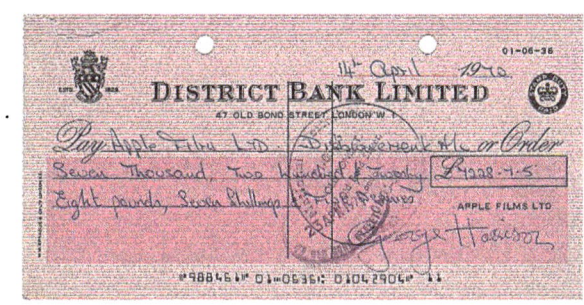

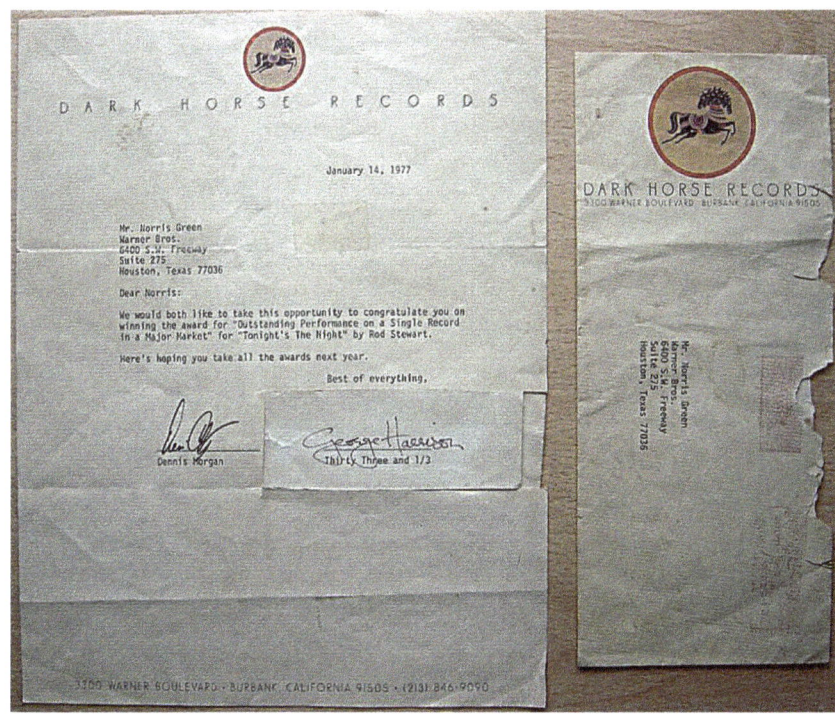

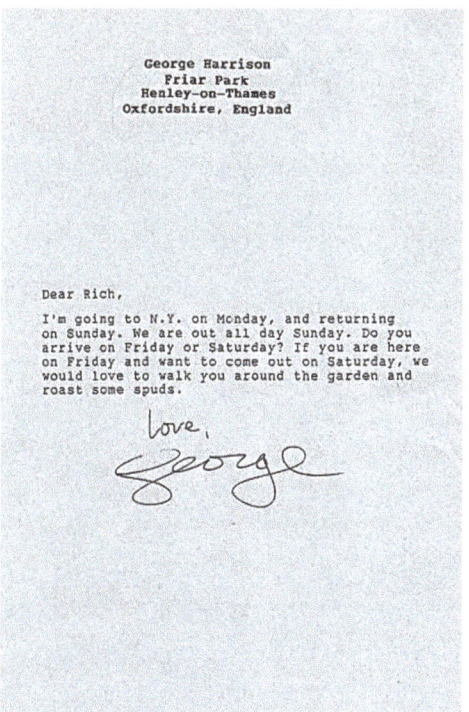

THE SOLO YEARS: CHECKS, DOCUMENTS, LETTERS, AND RECEIPTS

GEORGE HARRISON

A 1974 tour book from George's US tour with Ravi Shankar and Billy Preston, signed and dedicated on the inside by George who also has drawn the Sanskrit symbol.

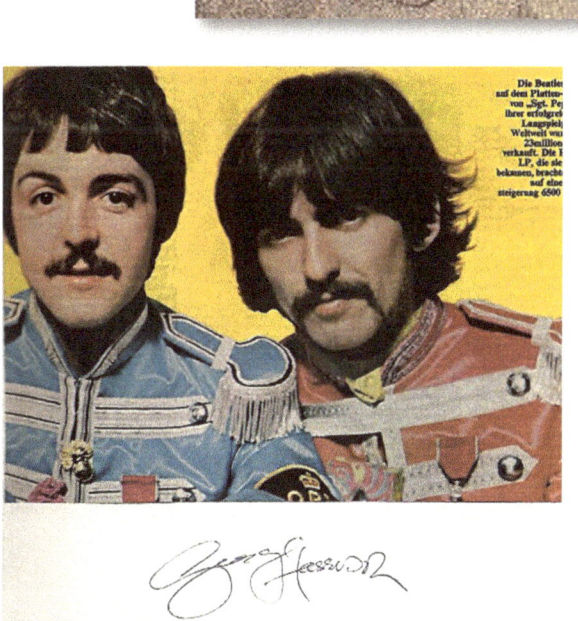

A nice signature of George that a lucky fan received back in the mail.

GEORGE HARRISON

Original "Let it Be" promotional photo signed by George in late 1970s.

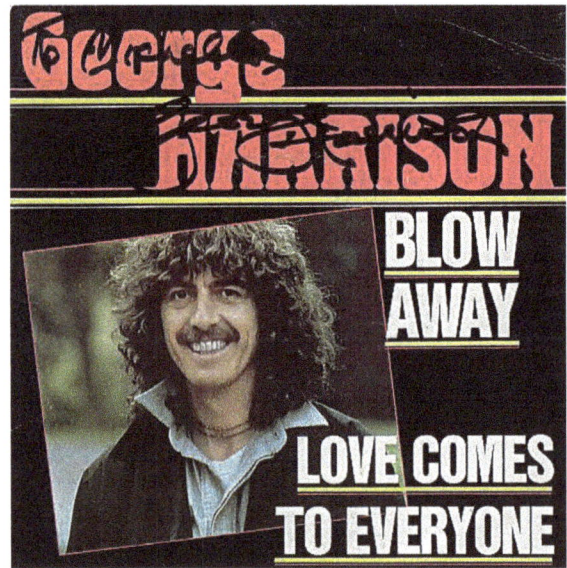

A menu for a flight from Los Angeles to London, signed with dedication to lucky fans on August 10, 1975.

Picture sleeve for "Blow Away" and "Love Comes to Everyone," signed with dedication by George in 1979.

George was a big race fan and attended many races over the years. He released the single "Faster" and he has signed nicely on the 45 picture sleeve.

In 1981 George Harrison released his album *Somewhere in England,* featuring the song in tribute to John Lennon, "All Those Years Ago." I was fortunate to have in my collection the signed album and the 45 picture sleeve.

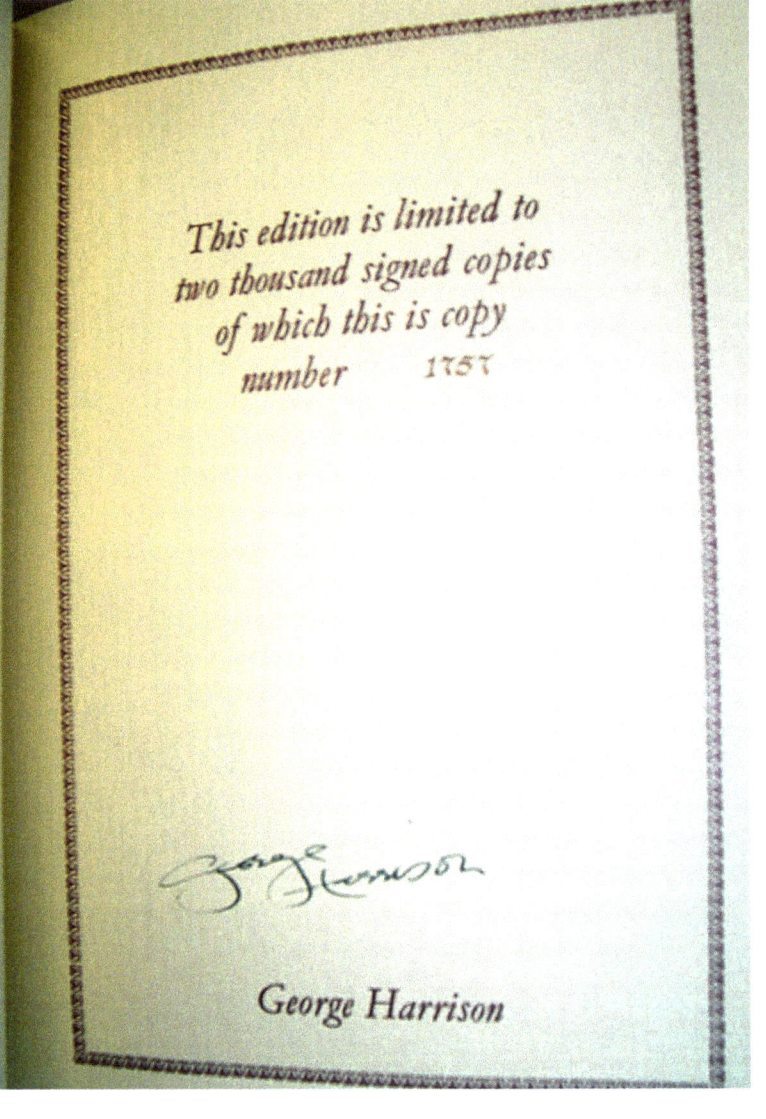

Genesis Publications Limited signed edition of George Harrison's book titled I Me Mine, signed by George and numbered 1757 of 2000 copies. Released in 1981.

A *Sgt. Pepper* album cover signed in the sky by George Harrison.

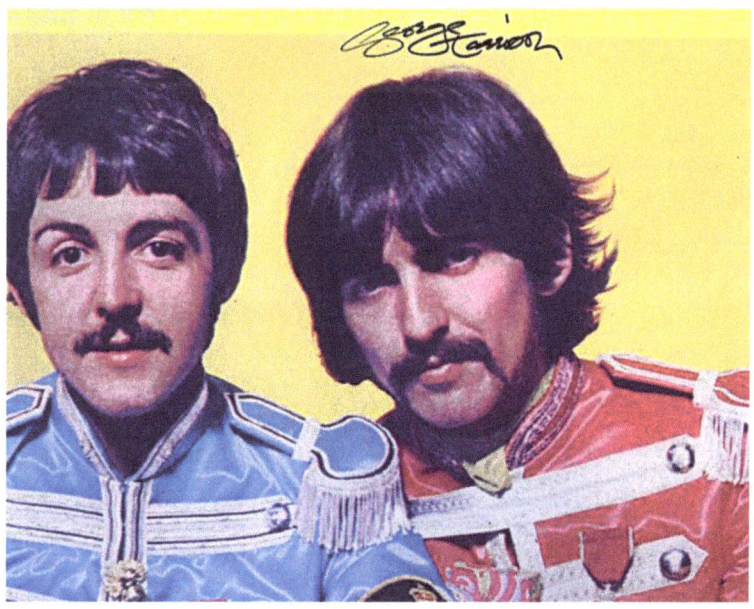

A *Sgt. Pepper* album cover signed by George Harrison above his image in the gatefold.

GEORGE HARRISON

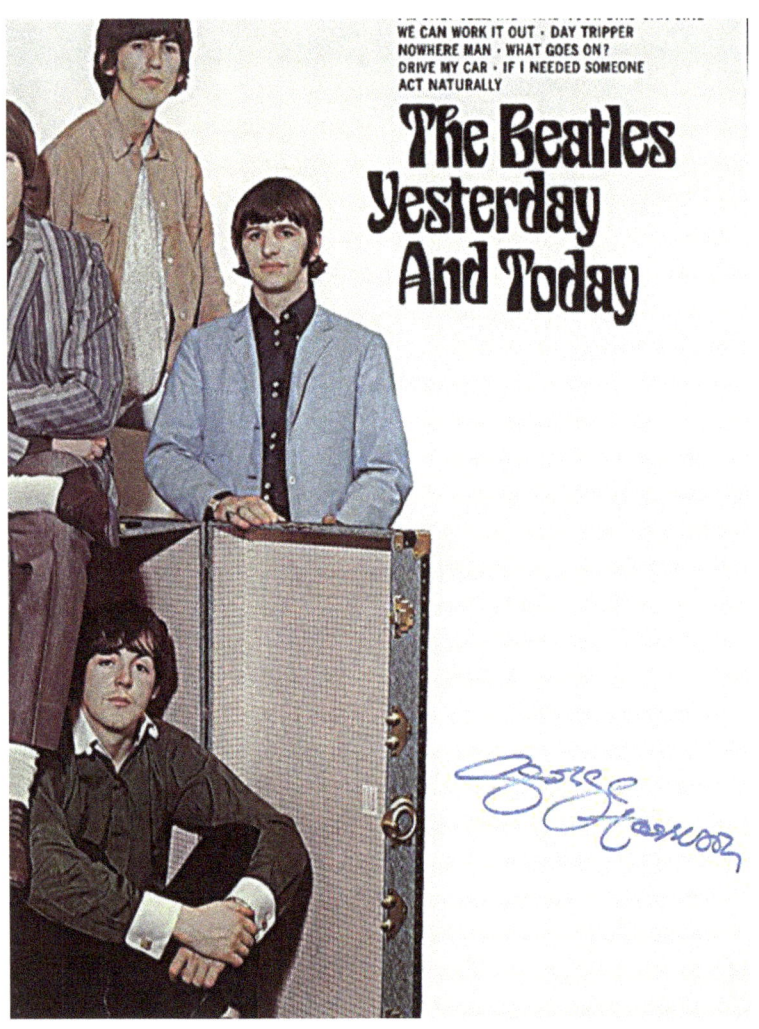

Yesterday and Today album covers signed by George Harrison obtained in Los Angeles.

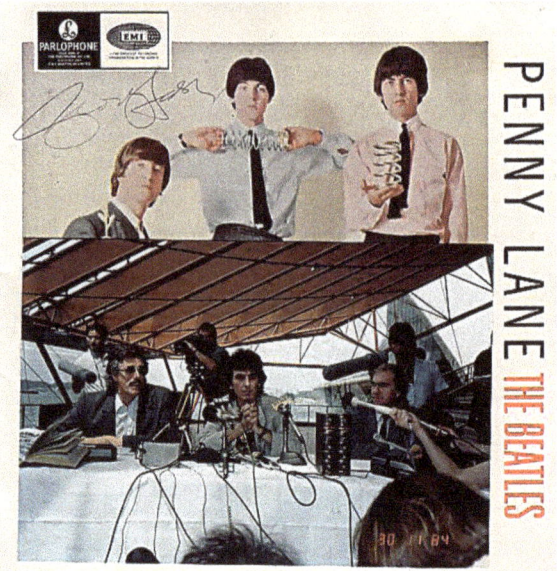

UK 45 cover for The Beatles song "Penny Lane" signed by George at a press conference in the 1980s. A photo of George with former Beatles press officer Derek Taylor from the signing accompanies.

The Best of Dark Horse album proof signed by George Harrison from 1989.

Help! album cover signed by George Harrison obtained in Los Angeles.

In 1987, Genesis released 3 lithographs of artwork relating to George Harrison's songs Taxman, Piggies and the most sought after one titled Here Comes the Sun, signed by George and artist, Keith West.

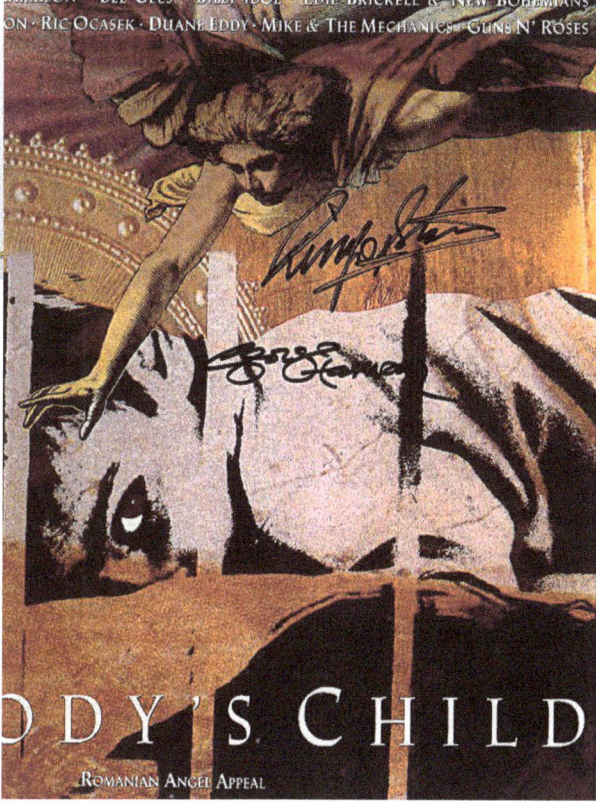

Nobody's Child: Romanian Angel Appeal was a charity album released in 1990 to benefit Romanian orphans, under the auspices of the Romanian Angel Appeal Foundation. Many artists donated songs. This album is signed by George Harrison and Ringo Starr.

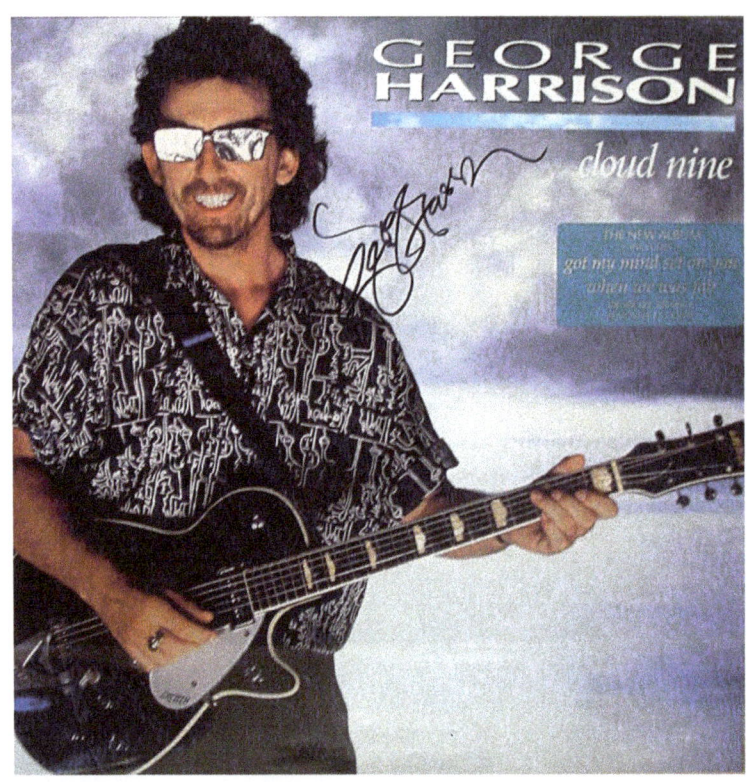

In 1987, George Harrison released *Cloud Nine* that garnered critical claim and featured many singles. Here are two album covers signed by George.

GEORGE HARRISON

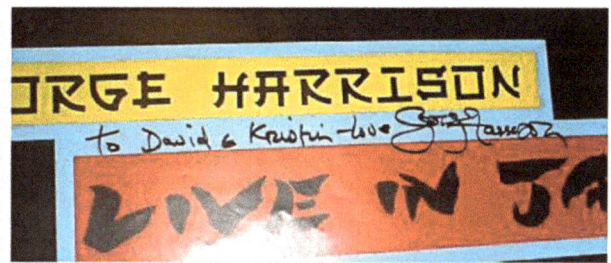

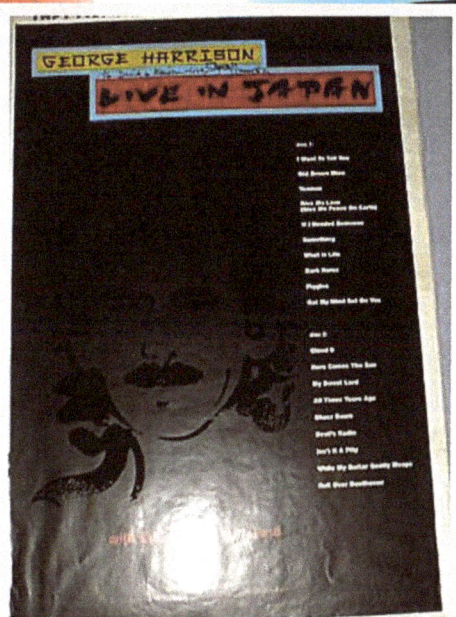

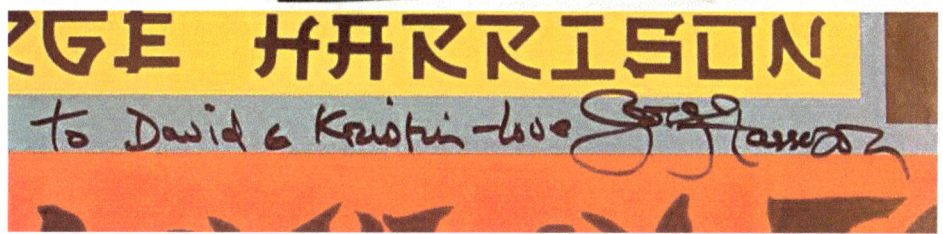

A promotional Poster for George Harrison Live in Japan signed and dedicated by George. This is George's second official live album release and was recorded during his joint tour of Japan with Eric Clapton in December 1991. The album was released in July 1992.

GEORGE HARRISON SIGNS FOR FANS THRU THE YEARS

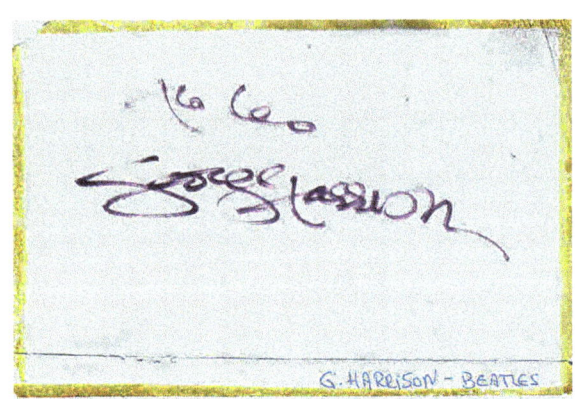

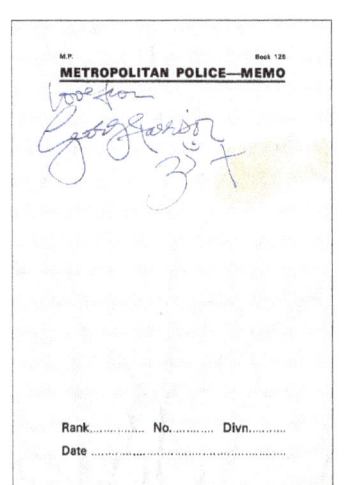

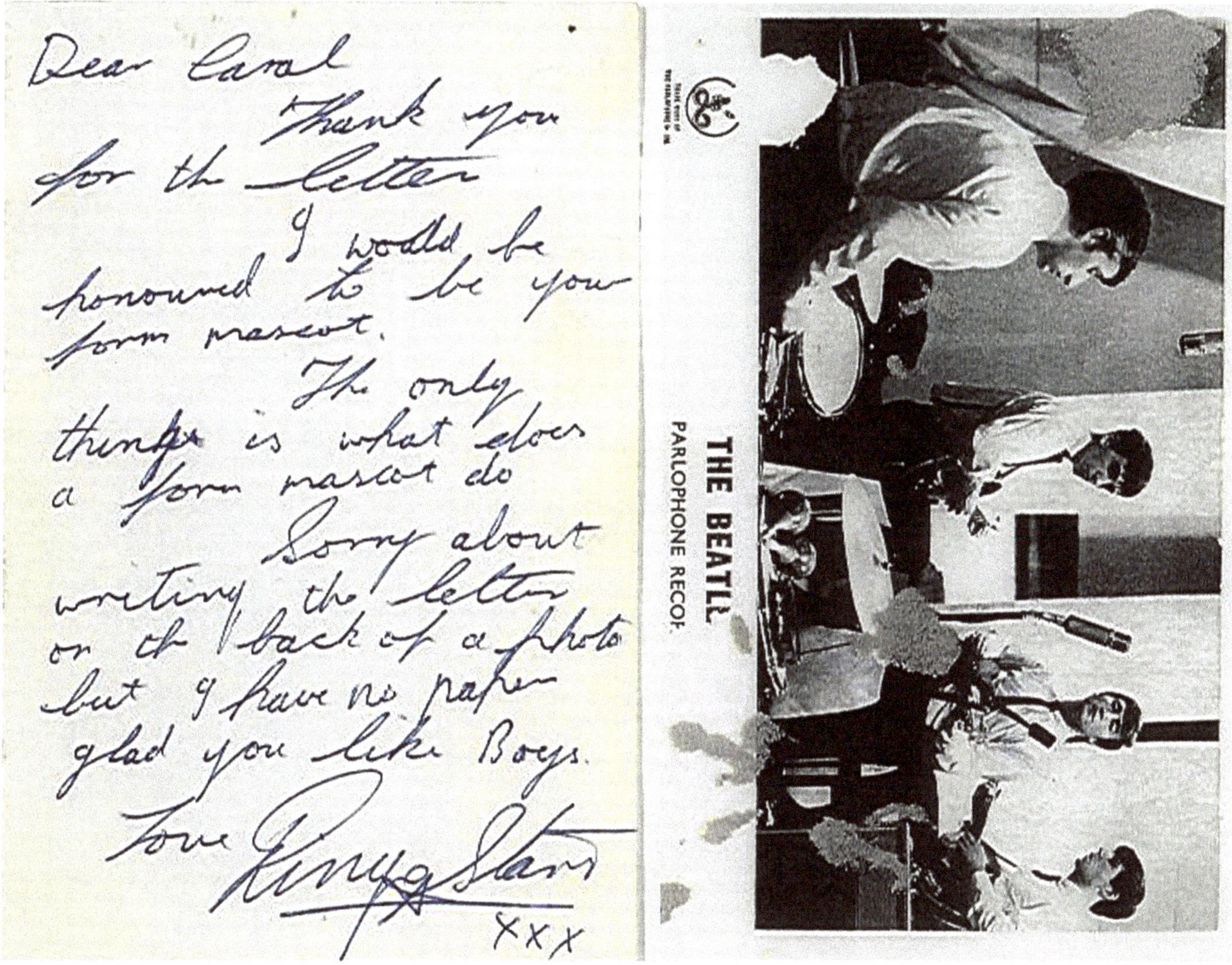

RINGO STARR

A nice handwritten and signed note to a fan from 1963 by Ringo Starr. Signed on the back of a Beatles photo Parlophone Card.

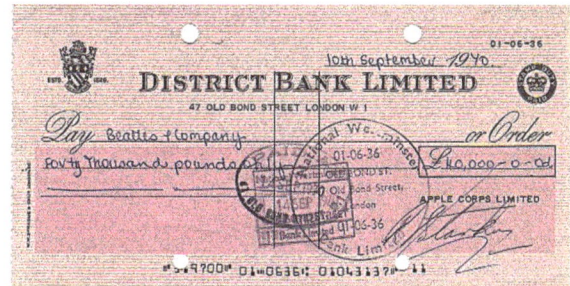

A District Bank Limited check payable to Beatles & Co. written in another hand and signed by R Starkey, which is Ringo's real last name. Check is dated September 10, 1970.

A National Westminster Bank Limited check payable to Ray Connelly written in another hand signed by R Starkey which is Ringo's real last name. Check is dated from March 1972.

➢ 151

UK pressing album cover for *With The Beatles* album, signed in 1964 on the reverse by Ringo Starr.

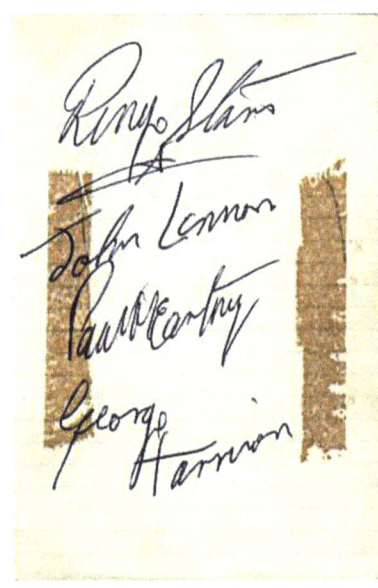

Every now and then, when the other three Beatles were not present at an autograph request, each Beatle would sign for the other three, as in this case with Ringo signing for the others.

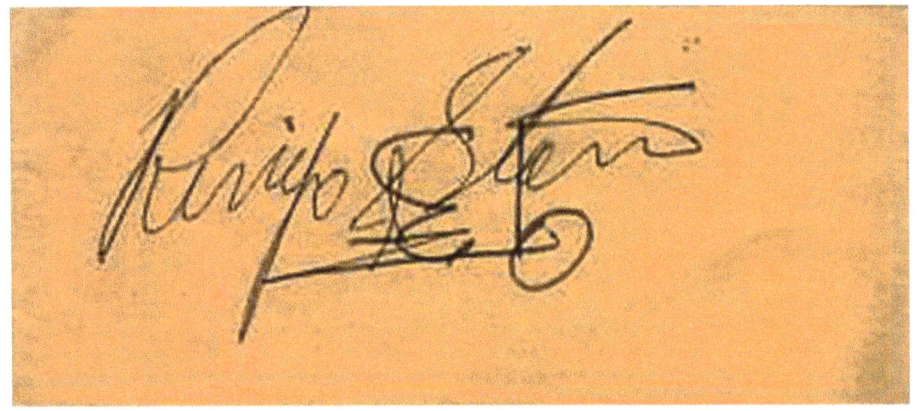

A West Coast Premiere movie ticket for the movie *That'll Be The Day*, released in 1973, with Ringo co-starring with rocker David Essex. Ringo signed the ticket on the reverse.

RINGO STARR

A money/loan request TLS by Ringo to Wobble Music Ltd., signed R Starkey from 1975.

A program from a show that Ringo attended has been signed by Starr and members of The Bee Gees, from 1970.

A color magazine photo attached to a white piece of paper sent to Ringo, requesting an autograph. He graciously signed the right side of the page.

A color Beatles trading card signed by Ringo Starr obtained by mail.

A lucky fan was at the right place at the right time, as they obtained Ringo Starr's signature on the reverse of a boarding pass in the 1970s.

➤ 153

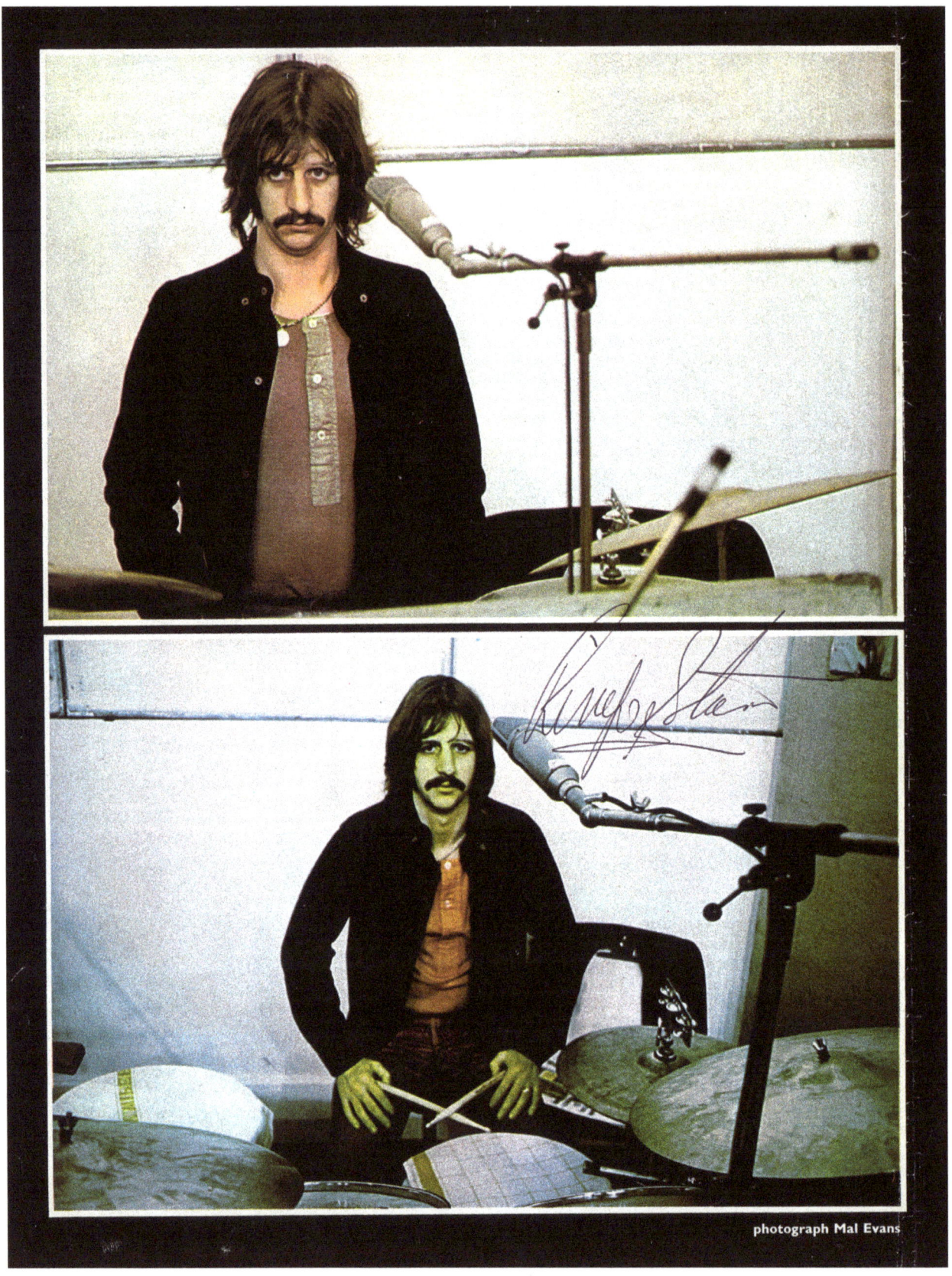

A photo page from *The Beatles Get Back* book signed by Ringo Starr to the right of his image in the 1970s.

A 45 picture sleeve of the song "Wrack My Brain" from 1981, signed by Ringo obtained through the mail.

A promotional 8x10 of Ringo from the movie *Caveman*, signed by Ringo Starr. The film was released in 1981.

A snapshot photo taken from the television, picturing Ringo in a film he co-starred in — the made for TV movie, *Princess Daisy,* in 1983. Ringo signed the photo, which was mailed to him.

The *Ringo* album cover signed by Ringo Starr on the front cover.

RINGO STARR

The Beatles *White Album* signed and dedicated by Ringo Starr on the front by the embossed title along with the poster from the album also signed by Ringo in the 1980s.

RINGO STARR

A season's greetings card to Ringo's stepfather, Harry, signed by Ringo and wife, Barbara Bach.

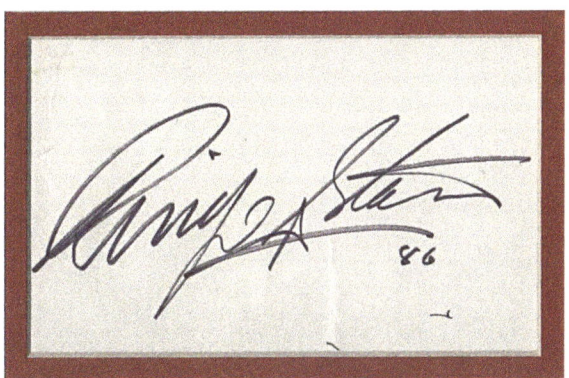

A nice signature of Ringo Starr, which he dated 1986, on a 3x5 index card.

A Shoney's restaurant menu signed on the front in the 1980s by Ringo Starr.

A large Ringo Starr signature on an 8 1/2x11 piece of paper.

A picture sleeve of "You're Sixteen," signed nicely by Ringo Starr. The signature was obtained during his 1989 All Starr Band tour.

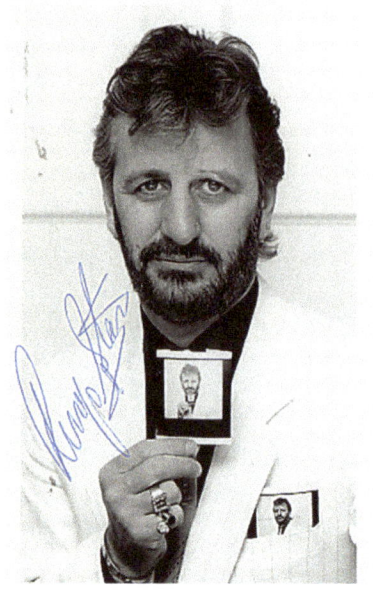

A handout photo card Ringo signed and sent in the mail to his fans who requested an autograph.

A promotional 8x10 photo signed by Ringo Starr with full name.

A nice full signature autographed drumhead by Ringo Starr from 1992. Later that year, he stopped signing his full name.

Ringo Starr and his All Starr Band tour program signed on front by Ringo and other the all star band members, along with actors Jack Nicholson, Gary Busey and musician Tom Petty, who attended the Los Angeles concert.

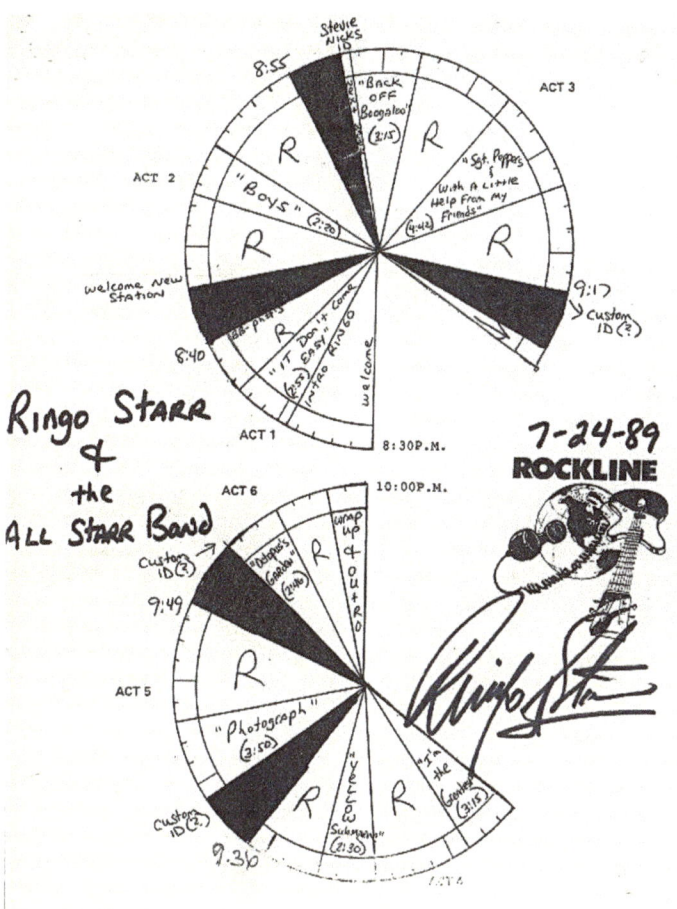

A *Rockline* time sheet in which Ringo appeared promoting his All Star Band Tour. He has signed the sheet, dated July 24, 1989.

A drumhead signed and dated by Ringo Starr in 1992.

A nice photo of The Beatles circa 1967, signed by Ringo with an added a star.

Dear George,

Happy Happy Birthday. Have a wonderful day and have one ppapaya on me.

Love, Ringo xxx

A very rare fax from Ringo to George Harrison, wishing him a Happy Birthday in Hawaii.

A small drumhead signed by Ringo Starr in the early 2000s.

An autographed drumhead, signed by Ringo who has dated it 1995.

A promotional jacket for Ringo Starr's All Starr Band Tour, signed nicely with a large signature on the arm of the jacket by Ringo, who also added a star.

A drumhead signed by Ringo Starr in 2003.

The Beatles *Yesterday and Today* album cover signed on the front by Ringo Starr in the 2000s.

The *Beatles 65* album cover signed on the front by Ringo Starr in the 2000s.

In October 2008 Ringo Starr made an announcement that he will no longer sign autographs. Except for charity events, he has held to his word.

Stuart Sutcliffe—
The Forgotten Beatle

Stuart Sutcliffe was born in Edinburgh, Scotland in 1940, and grew up in Liverpool, England. He attended Liverpool Art College and was regarded as one of the best painters in his class. It was there he met fellow classmate, John Lennon. They became friends and shared a room together. This is when John asked Stu to buy a bass so he could join a band with friends Paul McCartney and George Harrison. Stu could barely play but John wanted him in the band.

In September of 1960, while playing clubs day and night, Stu met photographer Astrid Kircherr. They fell in love quickly and she became his fiancée two months into the relationship. While there, Astrid gave Stu a mop top haircut and the rest of the band soon followed which would later be known as The Beatle Haircut.

However, on December 5, 1960, Harrison was sent back to Britain for being under-age. McCartney

and Best were also deported for attempted arson at the Bambi Kino, which left Lennon and Sutcliffe in Hamburg. Lennon took a train home, but Sutcliffe was sick and stayed in Hamburg. On January 20, 1961 Sutcliffe flew back to Liverpool but returned back to Hamburg in March 1961, with the other Beatles. Stuart wanted to be with Astrid and continue painting. In July, of that year, Sutcliffe decided to leave the group to continue painting.

While in Germany, Sutcliffe began experiencing severe headaches and acute sensitivity to light, which left him to temporary blindness. In 1962, Sutcliffe collapsed in the middle of an art class in Hamburg he did seek medical treatment but the doctors could not find reasons for the headaches. After getting checked in Britain with the same diagnosis, he returned to Hamburg where he was staying Astrid.

Stu and John signed by photographer Jurgen Vollmer. (IMAGE FROM THE DIE BEATLES IN HAMBURG POST CARD SET.)

Stu, John and George signed by photographer Astrid Kirchherr. (IMAGE FROM THE DIE BEATLES IN HAMBURG POST CARD SET.)

His condition worsened and after collapsing again on April 10, 1962, he was taken to hospital by Kirchherr (who rode with him in the ambulance), but he died before the ambulance reached the hospital. The cause of death was revealed to have been a cerebral hemorrhage causing bleeding in the brain.

On April, 13, 1962, Kirchherr met the group at Hamburg Airport telling them that Sutcliffe had died a few days before. They were stunned, especially John.

Stuart Sutcliffe influenced The Beatles in many ways and most people may not even know who he was in Beatle history. He was incredibly talented as an artist, a gentle soul and Astrid's and John's best friend who left the world way too early at the age of 21.

STUART SUTCLIFFE

An extremely rare handwritten letter envelope addressed by Stuart to his fiancée Astrid Kirchherr in Hamburg, Germany. On the reverse he has penned 'From Your Stuart". It is postmarked from Liverpool, January 28, 1961.

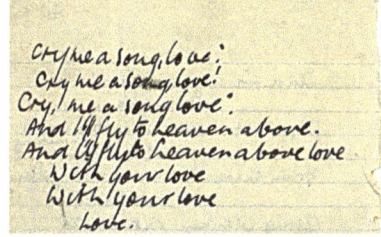

Handwritten poetry by Stuart Sutcliffe.

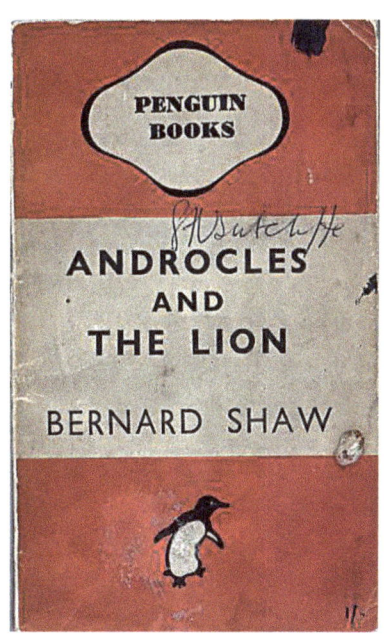

Stuart Sutcliff's personally owned and used book, Androcles and The Lion, with Stuart's signature on the front cover.

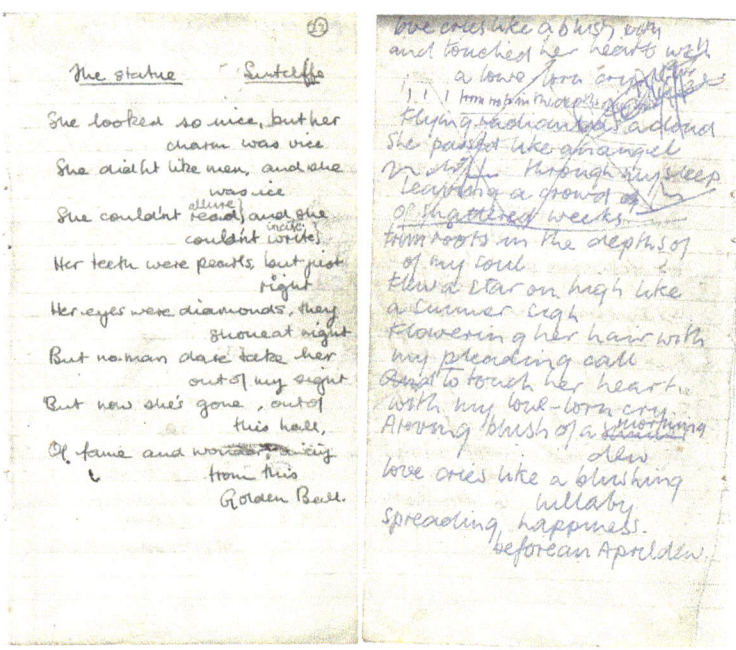

Interesting to note, Stuart had at least two different examples of handwriting, as you see in these images. Note both items came from the same poetry book owned by Stuart. If you look carefully, he has also written his last name, Sutcliffe, over the cross-outs.

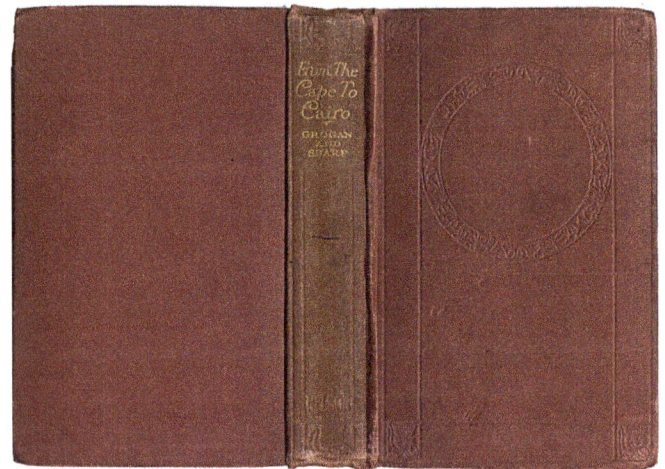

Stuart's personally owned and used book titled, *From the Cape to Cairo,* with Stuart's signature on inside cover.

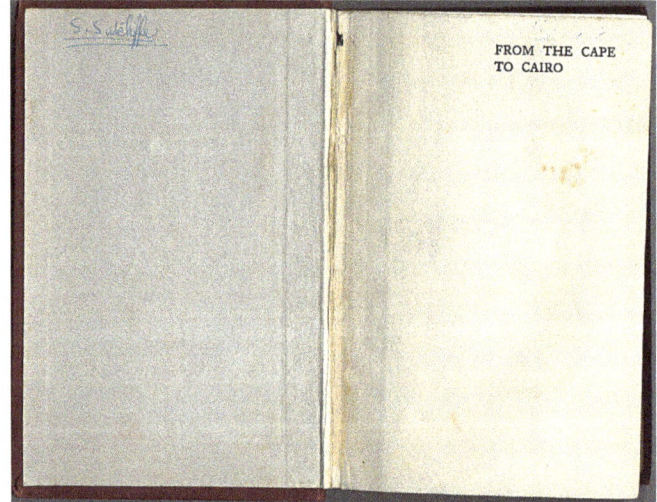

Eiplogue

I hope you enjoyed strolling down memory lane and viewing a very special history of the Beatles and their solo years in script and images. This was just a sampling of the items from many artists I collected over the years. More will be featured in future Lifetime Collections volumes, so stay tuned!

If you enjoyed this book, please check out *Rare, The Memorabilia Collection of a Lifetime,* which features historical items from my current collection. Readers will enjoy this book's incredible photography and the personal stories and details of the back stories of many of the items.

The deluxe coffee table edition of *Rare* is available on Amazon.com, and the standard edition can be found on most online bookstores, including Amazon.com and BarnesandNoble.com

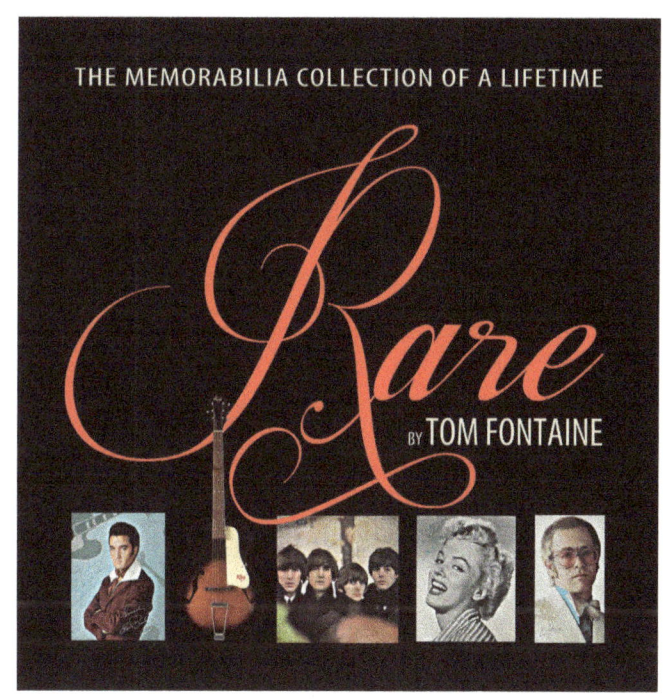

I would love to hear from you. All the best,

Tom Fontaine

For more information about The Tom Fontaine Memorabilia Collection, please visit my website:

Tjfontainecollection.com